CW00459188

ASPECTS OF BEING

ASPECTS OF BEING

Vivienne Cameron

The Book Guild Ltd
Sussex, England

The Book Guild Ltd
25 High Street,
Lewes, Sussex

First published 1997
© Vivienne Cameron, 1997
Set in Times
Typesetting by Acorn Bookwork, Salisbury

Printed in Great Britain by
Bookcraft (Bath) Ltd, Avon

A catalogue record for this book is
available from the British Library

ISBN 1 85776 160 X

CONTENTS

This book is dedicated with *agape* and gratitude to Dr Raymond Flood B.Sc., M.Sc., Ph.D., FIMA, University lecturer in mathematics and computer studies at the department for Continuing Education, Oxford University, whose inspired and inspiring seminars and encouraging tutorials led me into the fringes of scientific fields I would certainly not have attempted alone (excluding, I hasten to add, mathematics – of which I am resigned to remain in ignorance).

PREFACE

I was at school for only five years from the age of nine, my mother having by then taught me the basics of reading, writing, arithmetic and music to a good standard for a child of that age. After that, having attended six different schools, I cannot recall encountering one teacher who inspired me or was even adequate as a mentor. I was relieved to take my first step to independence with no higher expectations than to make a modest living by sitting at a desk pounding a typewriter. I was pleased to escape from that during World War II, only to find myself in khaki sitting at a desk pounding a typewriter. One marriage and three sons later I went back to work to keep my children fed and found myself (you guessed) sitting at a desk pounding a typewriter.

Things improved when I met my second life-partner, who helped me to realize that 'he who dares wins'. So I took out a bank loan I could not afford in order to do a house conversion and twice barely escaped bankruptcy, which caused a few sleepless nights. I took the first year of an apprentice painting and decorating course at the then Brighton School of Art to enable me to cope with a variety of workmen, most of whom found it difficult to believe that a female could do more than a cleaning job.

For many of us, while battling through the different challenges which life throws at us, there is an undercurrent, a feeling perhaps expressing itself in a state of dissatisfaction, or a need to search for meaning and which eventually comes to the surface; and so it was for me. A horror of organized religion and an interest in the fashionable philosophies of the day held me in the ranks of atheism for perhaps thirty years, until I came across the Gurdjieff teachings, especially the *Psychological Commentaries on the Teachings of Gurdjieff & Ouspensky* by the Jungian psychologist Dr Maurice Nicoll. But what initially drew me irresistibly towards the system of self-discovery was its formidable exponent,

P.D. Ouspensky's remark, 'You must not believe anything.' This I could not resist.

Aspects of Being is a compilation of some of the things which have excited my interest and proved to be important to me. I write in the hope that they may be of interest, too, to those who read it, and also that they may feel tempted to explore some of them further than I have been able to do. Should this be the case, I would be delighted to hear about it.

INTRODUCTION

As I was reading about the new theory of chaos, it began to look more and more possible that young scientists had, for some time, been engaged in unveiling, bit by bit, the mysterious creative force which great religions have posited for centuries. The Hindu teaching regarding Brahma, Vishnu and Shiva (the creator, the maintainer and the destroyer) came easily to mind. This teaching begins with a Prime Mover – Brahman – who created the whole universe including, of course, the three gods, the creative, sustaining and dissolving forces. This clearly implies that creativity is an ongoing process, otherwise there would be no role for Brahma to perform. An automatic, static kind of world is, therefore, no part of the Hindu scheme of things.

Although there are various views about Shiva's function, it has to be conceded that without the destroyer there would be no room for creativity. The Buddhist scholar, Lama Govinda, says that the Hindus have got it slightly wrong and that Shiva should be called the transformer – the dynamic principle in cosmology. Whoever is right, the important thing is this reminder of a well-established law: the ability of matter to synthesize by way of a catalyst which works, often unnoticed, in situations variously described as positive/negative, active/passive, *yin/yang*, masculine/feminine, which appears to enter all fields and to be unceasingly at work. So we may interpret turbulence and orderly movement as being two aspects of a three-fold process, and the hidden order in chaos as being the catalytic third.

The US philosopher, Renée Weber, talks of the *Svetasvatatara Upanishad*, one of the Hindu holy books, with its enigmatic metaphor of creation: 'Like the butter hidden in the cream is the [source] which pervades all things.'

Here, she says, is a creation myth of surprising elegance. It accounts for all diversity by means of one principle, transforming itself out of its own ground. In Indian cosmology, the phenomenal

xi

world is the solid, the precipitate, which becomes crystallized in space and time by the cosmic consciousness in which it floats. I am struck by the economy of the model which accounts for all the diversity in the universe by evoking one single principle, transforming itself into density and visibility out of its own subtle ground.

She goes on to point out its close kinship with the schema of the dense and subtle matter of physicist David Bohm's implicate order, which is hidden from the explicate order of the world we experience. His theory, with its states of enfoldment in the implicate order and of its unfolding, in the explicate order, is in line with certain chaotic behaviour discovered by Cartwright and Littlewood while studying forced oscillations (see Chapter 1).

Rupert Sheldrake, whose main interest is in biological genesis, postulates, in his book *A New Science of Life*, the existence of an all-embracing 'morphogenetic' field which forms and develops both organic and inorganic structures, these structures being connected by what he terms 'morphic resonance'. He makes the plea that we should stop referring to 'The Laws of Nature', that phrase being merely a political metaphor. 'In an evolutionary universe,' he explains, 'why not think of laws developing in time, just as real human laws do, evolving as new precedents arise?' He suggests we should talk, instead, of 'Habits of Nature' which evolve, rather than of the invisible, intangible laws that 'happened to be there in the first place'.

Ongoing creativity needs not only freedom to develop but also a structure in which to operate, and chaotic behaviour seems to indicate that there is such an underlying foundation which controls and at the same time gives opportunity for change.

Warwick University's mathematician Ian Stewart says, 'One of the characteristic features of chaos is that tiny errors propagate and grow.' The language he uses is interesting, giving the impression, whether intentional or not, of a living organism comparable with mutation in the vegetable and animal spheres.

All the foregoing views have in common the idea of some kind of creative process. The aspects of being which I have attempted to highlight throughout this book are not *just* aspects of being, but of *being* and *becoming*. It is my belief that we, as unique individuals, are in the process of creating ourselves, and that what we become is very much up to us. We may be extremely minute specks compared with the astronomical size of the universe, but *creative* specks, nevertheless, and if you bear with me to the last chapter, whether you will agree with me or not, I hope you will understand why I say that we, too, have the opportunity to transform ourselves out of our own ground in this evolutionary universe.

1

THE SCIENCE OF EARTH

A LAYMAN'S VIEW OF CHAOS THEORY

James Gleik, in his very readable book *Chaos*, comments that twentieth-century science will be remembered for just three things: relativity, quantum mechanics and chaos. As one physicist put it to him,

> Relativity eliminated the Newtonian illusion of absolute space and time; quantum theory eliminated the Newtonian dream of a controllable measurement process; and chaos eliminated the Laplacean fantasy of deterministic predictability.

Even if we are a mite hazy about the Newtonian dream and have little idea what the Laplacean fantasy could be, we get the message – chaos theory is very important to scientists. But why should it make any difference to us? One reason is that it is a very down-to-earth theory based on observations of physical systems. A physical system is merely a name scientists give to parts of the environment such as a cloud, a tree, a body of water and so on. The second reason is that eventually scientific ideas trickle down into everyone's thinking. We take for granted things which would have been dubbed witchcraft, or worse, in previous centuries: the transmission and reception of sound waves over long distances, and the fact that things are no longer regarded as solid, but are made up of little units of energy

1

whizzing round so fast as to give the illusion of solidity. We now know that we live in an unpredictable world where previously we thought that, if only we knew all the facts, we would be in complete control of everything.

In the late 1970s physicist Robert Shaw was at the Santa Cruz campus of the University of California when he became founding member of the little group of young men who gathered round him. They had quite different interests, but what initially drew them together was a common interest in and knowledge about computers, before such a tool had begun to be taken seriously. Ignored by the establishment, they had to scrounge around for premises and equipment and were to wait a full two years before gaining grant status. None of this proved to dampen their enthusiasm, and they named themselves The Dynamical Systems Collective. Less grandly, others later dubbed them The Chaos Cabal.

They spent their time studying how the world works – not the tidy, regular movements of linear systems which could easily be put into simple equations, but the untidy, obstreperous movements which things make when they get out of control and become thoroughly unpredictable; such things as patterns of smoke, cloud formations and pendulum swings when they go haywire, even statistical fluctuations – anything at all at the stage when it appeared to get out of control.

All such phenomena had, up to that time, been ignored by scientists as being irrelevantly abnormal or, indeed, because they were not noticed at all. This was an extraordinary time for these variously specializing scientists, as they began to uncover different facets of the subject, and to grow more aware of the others' work. Their discoveries grew steadily, largely unnoticed, into what was to become known as chaos.

Slowly and painstakingly, they began to penetrate various examples of apparently chaotic behaviour and to find complicated pockets of hidden order which appeared to attract any out-of-control phenomenon and to guide it into a new pattern. It was assumed there must be something there to cause the attraction, so, reasonably enough, the 'something' was named an *attractor*.

Attractors work in a number of ways. Some encourage a

system to change its direction; some to collect material at a central point, while others do the opposite and disperse it. Some systems seem to be taken prisoner and are made to circle round and round like a donkey on a treadmill. So what all this means is that physical systems of all kinds are either (1) behaving in an orderly fashion, (2) are breaking out of that orderly behaviour into turbulent randomness, or (3) are being pulled into a new, ordered state. Like dancers, they can do a stately minuet, join hands in a circle dance or go berserk, break away from their patterns and rush madly about until they find another dance which attracts them more.

There are various types of attractors, each bearing a name which gives the clue to its function. A *limit cycle* causes a system to go round and round, unless and until rescued by turbulence. A *sink* pulls a system into its basin, as it spirals inwards before coming to a stop. A *source* instigates the opposite behaviour, sending outwards that which comes within its reach, as does a spring of water.

Much more interestingly, there are *strange attractors* which do not fit into any of the above categories, and are strange in the sense of unknown, although it *is* known that they obey certain rules. A strange attractor never crosses its own path, neither does it travel the same route twice. If these rules were broken the attractor would cease to be strange and become a mere limit cycle – or even a sink. Another quality it possesses is that somehow or other in a world of finite space it finds infinite space to perform an infinity of action.

One of the early workers on attractors was Edward Lorenz, a research meteorologist, who began to study the three-dimensional swings of a pendulum at the point where it loses regularity and starts to swing, apparently randomly, becoming seemingly impossible to track. But Lorenz was not to be so easily defeated. Ingeniously, he decided to concentrate on one section of all the possible paths it could take at one point in its swing, and so he metaphorically cut a section through it. He plotted each swing as a dot on what became known as *phase space*. His chosen section contained the entire range of possibilities at a moment frozen in time. As the swings multiplied, the dots (or points in phase

3

space) began to appear. He must have been surprised and delighted at what he found. Firstly, a pattern formed. Not only that but where gaps appeared in the pattern the pendulum seemed to 'know' and one by one the gaps started to fill. He found that the pendulum never went over exactly the same part of the phase space more than once. Finally, the resulting pattern was spectacularly beautiful, a kind of double spiral in three dimensions looking like a carnival mask or the wings of a butterfly. It became known as the *Lorenz attractor*.

Science has been enormously helped by the development of computers, which have made possible fast calculations which were out of the reach of previous generations, mathematicians then being limited to hand-written methods. Computers never get bored, so weather patterns could be fed to them repeatedly. The starting point of these patterns was changed each time by an infinitesimal amount with the expectation that the small differences would result in equally small differences in the weather predicted. Instead, it was found that these very tiny differences increased dramatically as a programme progressed. After a while it became evident that accurate long-term weather forecasts were not a practical proposition. Butterflies seem to be important in chaos. These small variations which speedily diverge so markedly came to be known as *the butterfly effect*.

Now that the importance of chaos has been realized, more and more funding is being allocated to its study, and many centres set up. Another change in attitude is an increasing tendency to react against reductionism in physics. No longer is separation into smaller and smaller parts considered to be a first priority. Increasingly, each manifestation is to be regarded as part of a cosmic whole moving in harmony. This tendency has been strengthened by the discovery of an underlying similarity between different scales of the same system. Self-similarity from the microscopic to the very large is known as the *fractal* quality.

There appear to be fractals wherever we care to look. For example, the complicated pattern of a bracken leaf is found, on magnification, to be uncannily replicated by each small frond. Another example which has been examined is a coastline, the uneven edge of which appears random. However, if a section is photographed and then blown up to various sizes, each example is found to be so similar to all the others that it is indistinguishable from them. If two differently-scaled pictures are compared, it is impossible to decide which is the larger and which the smaller scale.

All strange attractors have this fractal quality, which has been demonstrated so dramatically on computer screens, where the viewer gets the impression of being drawn into an Aladdin's cave of changing beauty as the picture is gradually enlarged, showing increasing complexity, but always maintaining the main elements of the original pattern. One of the strangest aspects of these pictures is their continuing definition. If a photograph is magnified sufficiently, it eventually loses definition and becomes fuzzy. Not so with these computer images. They stay clear at every stage.

It seems possible that there may be limits to the fractal influence on physical forms. So far, fractals have not been found in either the very largest astronomical systems, or in any at sub-atomic level.

The Lorenz attractor was the first of many which have so far been discovered, most through a computer programme, which gives great freedom to experiment. Each attractor has a distinctive pattern of its own, and is named either after its discoverer or because of its shape. The Hénon attractor is shaped like a banana, the Mandelbrot set became the Gingerbread Man, and Feigenbaum produced the Fig Tree. Mitchell Feigenbaum it was who made a leap in knowledge of attractors by finding the mathematical constant which covers them all.

Classical geometry and mathematics have many uses in measuring static forms and registering orderly movements. Scientists, however, found these methods of little use in accounting for the ever-changing shapes of chaotic systems. A different kind of geometry, i.e. topology, is needed, which ignores measurement and embraces changes of pattern while obeying certain rules.

In 1945, two mathematicians, Cartwright and Littlewood, set up an experiment to test the effect of a forced oscillation being added to a naturally-occurring one. This turned out to produce chaotic behaviour. The idea was later expanded by Stephen Smale, who used a horseshoe shape which he proceeded to stretch and fold repeatedly. It was soon realized that this iterated action was a basic process in chaos, which had also been used to produce the butterfly shape of the Lorenz attractor. Smale's horseshoe was a breakthrough and gave rise to a wealth of new ideas in the area of chaos.

Can it be coincidence that this chaotic stretching and folding reminds one so vividly of the David Bohm theory of implicate and explicate order, where the very fabric of existence is a series of foldings and unfoldings? The two theories, one referring to higher realms and the other basic to this one, make comfortable bedfellows, and simplicity is, after all, a quality beloved by scientists.

One particular aspect which I find very satisfying is the way in which scientists of many different disciplines were brought together by their common interest in chaos. Weather was Edward Lorenz's subject, Hénon was an astronomer and Mandelbrot a mathematician. There were also a physicist and a biologist.

The laws of chaos reach into the deepest recesses of being, both physical and mental – arguably into emotional and spiritual ones as well. Yet these laws are discernible in every area of life and matter, from star clusters to the particles of physics; from population swings to the varying incidence of infectious disease; from volcanoes to the beat of a butterfly's wings. Patterns form, trapped in steady states or helpless oscillations, until – from the shackles of order and predictability – they are liberated to behave randomly. Chaos allows complexity to flourish – complexity of pattern, of movement, not mere *being* but the growth activity of *becoming*.

Strange attractors are at work offering opportunities to try new patterns, opportunities not only for physical systems but surely also for individuals. Incomplete knowledge as yet gives a strange attractor a cloak of bizarre abstraction – seemingly infinitely tangled, but always secretly guiding and ordered.

On screen, graphic images – unerringly mimicking reality –

capture fantastic and delicate structures which underlie the complexity we hardly understand and which, to some, hint at higher intelligence, wisdom and purposive consciousness.

APPROXIMATELY 4.669

AN ENCOUNTER WITH CHAOS THEORY

A money-spider journeys purposefully across
The vastness of a hearthrug's rough terrain
Which humankind would straddle in one stride.
Man crosses cavalierly, without a second's thought.
What does either know of their subtle phase space world?

Reading, the head behaves chaotically,
Small islands of order forming in the mind.
The body carries on.
Cycles of dawn, day, dusk, dreams;
Activities, pauses; meetings, partings.

Amongst the semi-conscious mish-mash
Intriguing patterns –
Darting in and out of consciousness –
Refuse coordination.
Mysterious fractions of fractal dimensions
Defy old classifications.
Newly discovered scaled similarities
Fascinate and bemuse.

Still persists disruptive disorderliness
Of a brain bewitched by patterned pools.

Stretch and fold – stretch and fold –

Startling every mathematician
Magical numbers repeat unbidden.
An unexpected eigenvalue
Becomes (what else?) a *Feigenvalue.*

BEYOND CHAOS

During the period when the new theory of chaos dazzled us with the first stunning series of infinitely magnifying complex fractal patterns being displayed on computer screens, we learned that disorder was much more than a hiccup in that tidy Newtonian world of simple equations and meekly circling particles and planets. We began to accept the previously unthinkable – that wild weather was not just a storm in a teacup; that its disorderly non-linear conduct was somehow meaningful and that, for all its bluster, it knew how to keep a secret. It took young, lively minds and that new toy – the lowly computer (despised by all right-thinking scientists) – plus a modicum of luck, to begin to uncover the patterns behind chaos. Complicated patterns they were too, for all the simplicity of their genesis: beautiful realities of complex structures unfolding on the unreality of a man-made screen. What did it all mean? No one knew.

But obviously it could not rest there. As chaos theory gained its place in the scientific scheme of things it was natural that great minds should bend towards the big question, where did they come from – these pockets of order which seemed to manifest unbidden as do daffodil shoots in spring? *Why is it that the Second Law of Thermo-dynamics Fails to Hold Sway?* Why is entropy not causing us all to wind down like clockwork toys? Or, as Dr Mitchell Wardrop put it in a BBC programme *Anti-chaos* in November 1992, 'Why is there something rather than nothing? There is an enormous amount of structure in the world. It's almost as if there is a universal yearning for order – almost a *force* towards order.'

Once the fact was known that very simple initial conditions can give rise to all kinds of ordered, creative complexity, the way was open. That fact, like a gift from heaven, was the golden key which could open doors to further knowledge, and so a variety of research projects began. One, in the field of chemistry, mixed four different chemicals together, with the expectation that they would form a random group of molecules. Instead, a high degree of order was obtained, as concentric waves of alternating colours were observed. This was an almost unbelievable result, bearing in mind that billions of molecules were involved in the experiment.

Similarly-structured behaviours have been observed in other fields. For example, take the reproductive process of the slime mould (if you dare). Individual cells, previously going about their chaotic business without reference one to the other, suddenly swarm together like soldiers on a parade ground responding to a word of command. Or take birds – everyone is familiar with the sight of a flock of birds flying in formation, gracefully wheeling and turning in unison as if controlled by a single brain, when, only seconds before, they were flapping and generally cavorting in a very individualistic manner. Studies of this phenomenon have revealed that order travels like a wave through an entire flock in about one-seventieth of a second, which is far less than a bird's reaction time, and rules out any possibility of follow-my-leader type behaviour.

Researchers began to see this kind of contrasting behaviour in many areas. Sudden changes from chaotic, individualistic, random movements to group order were noticed in shoals of fish and in colonies of ants. Individual ants behaving randomly for a period suddenly stop as though the foreman has blown the whistle for tea break. This happens rhythmically every 28 minutes or so. Every group studied showed similar patterns. Each chemical, each slime mould cell, fish, insect, bird acted randomly, autonomously, not individually programmed to act in concert, yet, when a group became large enough, order emerged, apparently spontaneously. It became necessary to find new models to study this phenomenon, which came to be called *anti-chaos*, and research was undertaken using both controllable physical systems and computer models. One such was Brian Goodwin's computer 'ants'. Professor Goodwin, of the Open University, and colleagues made a simple computer model of an ant colony, representing them as automata which could move, react and interact but were *not* programmed to act in unison, and yet periodicities similar to those of the real ants were soon in evidence. The computer ants behaved like a real colony. It was also found that the initial random behaviour was an essential prerequisite. Without this key element *no order emerged*. It seems an astonishing and fascinating result: that automata on

10

computer, without being in any way programmed, other than to wander about and collide indiscriminately, developed an identical pattern of intermittent order as was found in a genuine colony, and that random movement was an essential ingredient to trigger that order.

A very simple physical model, which has been successfully employed, consists of sand being poured at a constant rate on to a flat surface. Observers find that at the beginning, while the sand is still more or less flat, there is stability. As the pile grows taller and larger it gets more and more unstable, breaking out into avalanches of various sizes occurring randomly in a completely uncoordinated manner. Then a critical point is reached where it cannot grow any higher and the behaviour changes radically. The avalanches disappear and the pile takes on and retains a symmetrical shape and constant size, the excess sand falling evenly away. At this stage, what is happening at any one point affects, and is affected by, what is happening at all other points, and it becomes a whole unit. Instead of a series of independent systems behaving individually, it becomes one integrated dynamical system.

Professor Stuart Kauffman of the Santa Fe Institute became interested in antichaos because of its apparent ability to throw light on life itself, life which had somehow emerged from the primordial soup of the early stages of the universe. It was his intuition and hope that the order evident in the development of cell differentiation would prove to be

spontaneous, natural and almost inevitable, rather than an improbable consequence of mutation and selection. I wanted to understand the order of development, the way a fertilized egg develops into an adult organism . . . it goes through 50 cell divisions...it winds up making about 250 cell types.

As all cells have a set of about 100,000 identical genes but finish up as 250 different varieties, it is relevant to ask how this cell differentiation could possibly occur. The answer is known to be in the timing of their periods of activity and inactivity. They differ not in structure but in the order in which they become

11

active. Professor Kauffman comments, 'They turn on and off in a sort of orchestrated dance.' So he had to devise a way of studying this on/off behaviour, and hit on the idea of an electrical system which could mimic the cells' behaviour by means of an array of light bulbs wired together with a switch which would obey a certain rule. It could be a rule such as that an individual light bulb lights only if two others are lit, this kind of system being known as a *Boolean network*.

Suppose it was worked out how long it would take to find order in this system by trial and error. Statistically speaking, in a system containing a mere 200 light bulbs it would take an astonishingly long time. In order to trawl through all the possible connections, it has been estimated it would take *billions of times longer* than the age of the universe. In fact, against these appallingly huge odds, unbelievably, the Boolean network of light bulbs did produce order.

In the case of genes, the number would be, not 200, but 100,000 per cell. Says Kauffman,

If each gene could be active or inactive...the number of possible alternative patterns in the genome of your body in any one of your cells is one followed by thirty thousand zeros. It's an enormous, hyperastronomical, unthinkable number. Antichaos says that a system of that kind, despite that vast complexity, boxes its behaviour into a tiny...region of its space possibilities and cycles through them. That's the order that's pointed to when one says antichaos.

Kauffman has for years felt intuitively that life is an expected property of complex chemicals; that it is 'spontaneous, natural and almost inevitable, and I think that is the case.' He calls it 'order for free', but order of a simple kind. There had to be a mechanism whereby simple cells could combine to form more complicated structures, and his theory to explain this involves the principle of catalysis.

A catalyst appears when two molecules meet, which encourages the two to combine rather than to drift apart again. But a further mechanism is needed to form all the different elements that go to make up the ingredients of life, and Kauffman's solution is to posit a process of autocatalytic sets, in which catalysis produces a chemical which then combines with the two already present to make a further catalyst. He says,

> If, in fact, life emerged as such collective autocatalytic sets of molecules, then it would appear to be the case that the routes to the formation of life are much more probable than we have expected; so that we might hope to find it, for example, on other promising planets and other solar systems. In fact, life is the consequence of broad boulevards of possibility and not the back alleys of thermodynamics and improbability.

Dr Chris Langton, also of the Santa Fe Institute, reported on other computer-based studies which aimed at simulating very simple parts which interact in a particular environment. These were based on cellular automata, which consist of grids of tiny squares, the squares' actions being dependent on neighbouring squares. Each cell is programmed with very simple rules which cause loops to be built up. As a loop completes its circuit it surrounds itself with copies which then create further loops. As soon as the original loop has no space left to produce, it 'dies' – apparently strangled to death by its progeny.
Dr Langton says,

> What I ended up with was something which is very reminiscent of the growth of trees...or as in the growth of a coral reef, where the outermost surface consists of living animals that have built their shells on the shells of dead ancestors.

Following recent detailed studies of the animals and plants inhabiting the rainforests, it became possible to create a whole computer ecosystem which has faithfully copied the patterns of actual ones. Computer universe inhabitants 'live' by two simple rules – *reproduce* and *mutate*. Rainforest experts confirmed similarities in behaviour with that of actual forests, with parasites emerging, only to have their energy stolen by other parasites, followed by a *status quo* during which mutual trust is achieved

13

for a time, until further cheats emerge – all very like the evolutionary cycle of life forms.

No one was prepared for the scale and diversity of the computer 'life' forms as they developed and became autonomously creative. Computer pictures show interesting and realistic shapes developing, giving the appearance of speeded-up photography of genuine vegetation. The inescapable conclusion is that it is immaterial which medium is employed or studied; whether based on computer bits or living cells, the same process is at work.

Perhaps the most impressive examples are not obviously physical at all – i.e. in such things as money supply and economics generally. But we have to remember that these systems are man-made, and that man is, after all, an animal species. It has been found that financial forecasts gleaned from computer programmes have been known to beat the stock markets *in the short term*, but in the long term, like weather forecasts, they are bound, by the laws of chaos, to fail.

An interesting example of individuals doing – not what they believe to be expedient – but what they deem to be ethical, i.e. in choosing morally acceptable investments for their money, has proved to be unexpectedly successful. The growth rates of their investments during a three year period have outperformed those of conventionally invested funds. Could that be a glimpse of spontaneous order? If so, increasingly ethical behaviour in all fields presumably would hasten the process of universal order, and the need for hierarchical government much reduced.

That celebrated US inventor/architect/philosopher, Dr R. Buckminster Fuller was a firm believer in the power of ethical action long before it was validated by scientific study. As a young man he became penniless in spite of all his efforts to provide for a wife and child. At that low point in his life he made a courageous decision which he never went back on. He vowed never again to attempt to make money, but to do only whatever he found needed doing and that no one else was attending to, in order to benefit as large a number of people as possible. From then on he led a phenomenally successful life in many fields, and money ceased to be a problem for him and

14

his family.

All this implies that universal principles of organization are at work, and that theories of randomness and progress by trial and error become less and less convincing. Just as it was found that chaotic behaviour spontaneously broke out from an ordered system, so in antichaos we now find order emerging spontaneously from what looked hopelessly structureless. Until recently, this concept was considered to be extremely unlikely, and Darwinian ideas of natural selection remained relatively unchallenged. Now, with patterns being found in so many different systems, we are bound to reconsider the whole question. Professor Goodwin's opinion is that 'the emphasis has shifted from natural selection as an external force to a robust dynamics of development as the generator of these forms.'

If evolution is a complex system inherent in every classification of form, then the concept of natural selection really would appear to be relatively unimportant. The implications of this are no less than staggering, and we have to face the fact that man can no longer regard himself as 'above' nature. It is necessary for us all to realize instead that we are merely a part of nature and are subject to exactly the same creative laws – whatever they may be – as the rest of the natural world.

Physically and geographically speaking, we think of systems as having some kind of stability, but this is an illusion. For instance, as with the sand pile example, the earth's crust is at a critical point of balance between random (or chaotic) behaviour and ordered (or antichaotic) behaviour. It has, over millennia, become a unified global system in a geographical sense, and finds its fine point of equilibrium in the balance between the two forces.

It has been found that all dynamical systems have similar growth patterns, the same sequence of events taking place whether it be, as we have seen, in the behaviour of living communities, or, for example, in the patterns of weather, or in the way civilizations rise, stabilize and finally collapse. All behave similarly, with comparable sequences of events.

Brian Goodwin points out that these are examples of what is

15

known as an emergent phenomenon; that is, the components exhibit one type of behaviour, but the system as a whole shows a quite different kind of behaviour. Thus it is not possible to reduce the behaviour of the whole to the behaviour of the individual components. 'You have a kind of irreducibility; and emergence refers to that kind of irreducible order that comes out of a complex system.'

This critical state of balance of the earth as a geographical unit is echoed by a similar state in which all living species contribute to a unified ecosystem – or did until man began behaving irresponsibly towards his own environment.

Now, perhaps, it is the turn of the human population to achieve the same state of critical balance, a technological revolution having opened the way to social, cultural and political intercommunication on a global scale. So far, man has managed to achieve pockets of order in various places in the world at various times, but until now, even if he had avoided polluting, pillaging and destroying, there would have been no opportunity to achieve worldwide intercommunicative equilibrium.

The population of the whole world has, for the first time in recorded history, the means to become a fully global dynamical system. This is not just possible, but seems inevitable if we accept that we are no more immune from the laws of antichaos than are the flocks of birds, the weather patterns and the rest.

We have to put the environment first because *we*, in common with everything else, *are* the environment.

As Buckminster Fuller proclaimed in his book *Critical Path*, whether we know it or not, whether we wish it or not, we are on that Critical Path. As we pass through the 'sand avalanches' of war, famine, slump, disease, which punctuate the lulls of success and prosperity, we should reach the end of these chaotic events, to be followed by the critical point of world order when, *for the first time ever*, man could be one global dynamical system; a system not imposed from the top layer of a political hierarchy, but emerging organically and naturally, in tune with the laws of spontaneous and inevitable order.

Now that there is scientific support for the concept that it should be happening, and that quite clearly it is not, we must

16

conclude that man is actively preventing this vitally important state of affairs from materializing, by his insistence on putting himself first and the environment last.

> The men of old, while the chaotic condition was yet undeveloped, shared the placid tranquillity which belonged to the whole world. At that time the yin and yang were harmonious and still; their resting and movement proceeded without any disturbance; the four seasons had their definite times; not a single thing received any injury, and no living being came to a premature end. Men might be possessed of the faculty of knowledge, but they had no occasion for its use. This was what is called the state of perfect unity. At this time, there was no action on the part of anyone – but a constant manifestation of spontaneity.
>
> A passage from the *Chuang-tzu*

The above paragraph from one of the most important Taoist books is quoted by Fritjof Capra in *The Tao of Physics*, and powerfully portrays an early period in the long process of man's development. This period is graphically modelled by the sand pile's early stages. The sand being comparatively flat, there were as yet no outbreaks of avalanches to disturb the idyllic tranquillity. However, without the growth of the pile to new heights, it would have remained completely dependent on its base with no shape or critical balance of its own. The state of balance and unity which it eventually attains would have been missing. On the other hand, if the base itself is rejected, the new unity can never be achieved. The base (the ground of being) and growth have to form a partnership to ensure success.

Man's overeagerness to become completely independent by rejecting the Ancient Wisdom has the effect of preventing him from achieving the very state which he desires. Capra puts the Taoist view:

> If one refrains from acting contrary to nature...one is in harmony with the Tao and thus one's actions will be successful. This is the meaning of Lao Tzu's seemingly so puzzling words, 'By non-action everything can be done.'

Man would surely not wish to go back to the placid tranquillity of the childhood of his race now that he has the opportunity to develop both racially and personally in new and exciting directions. Is it possible that the meek, after all, will inherit the earth? That does not seem a very attractive prospect, but we should consider the possible inaccuracies of translation, and the changes which occur in the meanings of words over the centuries. The word 'meek' in Middle English meant 'soft, gentle' as opposed to the present-day 'piously humble and submissive'. There is a lot to be said for making a soft approach and treating others gently if we aim at harmony. As for all the things people strive for – love, money, success, power – man's futile attempt to master the earth instead of taking his place within it, prevents him from receiving all he needs for his fulfilment. It seems we can leave it to the laws of hidden order to provide.

Mankind can choose to inherit the earth, but must be prepared to make one final sacrifice: the renunciation of power.

2

THE MATHEMATICS OF EARTH

There is an old Jewish joke about a rabbi who is visited by a wife, very upset at the behaviour of her husband.

At the end of her tale of woe she finishes, 'Rabbi, am I right?'

'You are right,' comforts the rabbi as she takes her leave.

Along comes the husband and tells his side of the story, finishing, 'Rabbi, am I right?'

'You are right,' said the rabbi, seeing his visitor out.

The rabbi's wife, unable any longer to pretend she had not been listening, exclaims, 'Husband, you told her *she* was right, and you told him *he* was right. They can't *both* be right, can they?'

Said the rabbi, 'You are right, my dear.'

The story came to mind as I considered the flowering of Greek civilization during the fifth century BC. Clashes of opinion often occurred and a philosopher of the time, one Democritas, seems to have had the same gift for appeasement of opposing views as had the rabbi.

This was a time when great changes in philosophical thought were taking place which were to echo down through the centuries. Sides were taken on such matters as the nature of atomic structure and whether the world was truly in a state of flux or if appearances were deceptive and reality was unchanging, immutable. Among the protagonists were, on one side Pythagoras and his followers, and on the other the Sophists. The latter were open-minded, forward-thinking and critical, not overly concerned with traditional beliefs and tending to approach mathematics in the context of morality and the study of the natural world, which they saw as a changing reality. In contrast, Pythagoras was a mystic as well as a philosopher and mathematician, and all Pythagoreans believed numbers to have a significance beyond the practical.

As to how open they were to new ideas is difficult to establish. The Sophists would have been wise to consider the possibility that eternal truths were hidden in the Pythagorean teachings, and in that respect seem not to have lived up to their reputation for open-mindedness. If all parties had listened to such as Democritas, and realized the others' merits as well as their own, history might well have taken a completely different course, giving the opportunity for synthesis instead of conflict to shape the world.

The belief that the entire universe could be explained in terms of numbers was fundamental to the Pythagoreans, number being at the centre of a cosmic philosophy which considered that all fundamental relations could be reduced to number relations. To put it another way, ratios between different aspects of form are said to control their action. Adherents to the theory do still exist, and many mathematicians have a deep feeling for the beauty of a mathematical proof. Physicist David Bohm, when Emeritus Professor at the University of London said, 'Somewhere behind the molecules there is something still more subtle which we call mathematics, which rules all that.'

I suggest it is reasonable to suppose that there might be clues to this knowledge in the Ancient Wisdom teachings, and on that assumption I decided to explore two symbolic forms and found them to be complementary in their messages, each in its own way throwing light on the other. This gave me sufficient information to construct a consistent set of six principles which are listed on page 32.

As I shall show, I have tested these principles on some physical systems, and also on the number classifications which mathematicians have devised over the centuries. In all cases, the examples conform to the six principles. This is true, as well, of one concerning chaos theory – the famous eigenvalue discovered by Feigenbaum. There are many areas worth exploration by someone with more knowledge than I possess, such as the ratios in light, colour and sound waves. Perhaps, also, in social groupings, remembering the optimum number theory.

The two forms I chose are the Sufi Enneagram and the Vedic Square. Magic squares have always been popular and were first used in ancient China, but were simply numbers arranged in such a way as to add to the same total, whether computed across the rows, down the columns or diagonally. The Vedic Square (see figures 2.1 and 2.1a) is of a different order. It is certainly symbolic, and I consider it may be a reflection of the use of number in earth energies. However it is viewed it gives information, one important factor being the method employed of adding numbers together until a single one is reached.

Take as an example the Feigenbaum eigenvalue mentioned above, which is so important in the mathematics of chaos. This number is 4.669 and, if my theory is correct, should be (Vedically speaking) a 7. My system calls for the numbers to be added as follows: $4 + 6 + 6 + 9 = 25$. $2 + 5 = 7$. Principle 6 says that 7 is the number which has the power to change form.

Figure 2.1

x	1	2	3	4	5	6	7	8	9
1	1	2	3	4	5	6	7	8	9
2	2	4	6	8	1	3	5	7	9
3	3	6	9	3	6	9	3	6	9
4	4	8	3	7	2	6	1	5	9
5	5	1	6	2	7	3	8	4	9
6	6	3	9	6	3	9	6	3	9
7	7	5	3	1	8	6	4	2	9
8	8	7	6	5	4	3	2	1	9
9	9	9	9	9	9	9	9	9	9

An ancient multiplication square designed by Islamic mathematicians.

The numbers are obtained by multiplying one of the figures in the top row by one in the first column. If the result is more than 9 the figures are added together until a single number is arrived at.

The geometrical patterns are the result of using one figure at a time wherever it appears in the square.

The Vedic Square

Note

It will be seen that

a) lines and columns have identical numbers

b) lines progress, of course, in agreement with the number of the line – ie. line 1 progresses in ones, line 2 in twos and so on. This is less apparent with the larger numbers as adding the numbers together masks the sequence, as in

7 14 21 28 35 42 49 56 showing as

7 5 3 1 8 6 4 2

c) as with geometrical pairs, all number relationships in the Vedic Square add up to 9. For example, 4 and 5 have:

4 8 3 7 2 6 1
5 1 6 2 7 3 8

d) diagonal lines all have symmetry. Also, complementary numbers total 9 in each case.

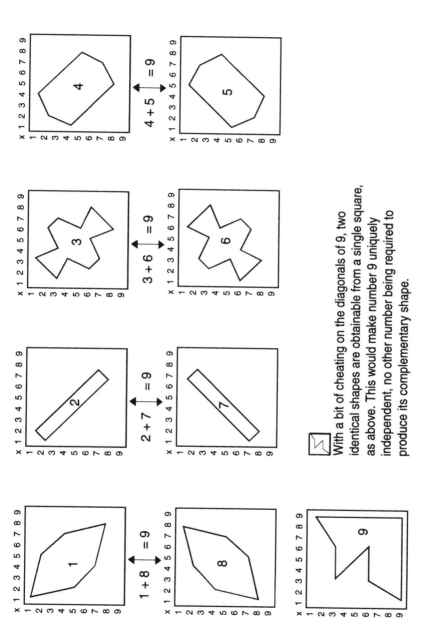

With a bit of cheating on the diagonals of 9, two identical shapes are obtainable from a single square, as above. This would make number 9 uniquely independent, no other number being required to produce its complementary shape.

4 + 5 = 9

3 + 6 = 9

2 + 7 = 9

1 + 8 = 9

Figure 2.1a   **The Vedic Square
complementaries**

1 and 8

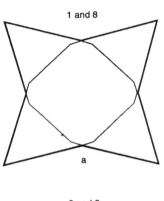

a

2 and 7

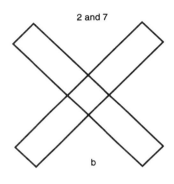

b

3 and 6

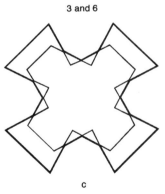

c

4 and 5

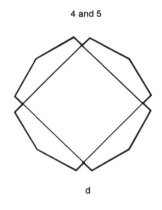

d

24

The Enneagram

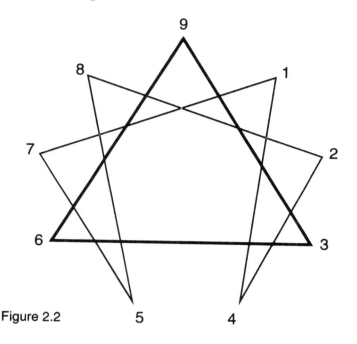

Figure 2.2

Ancient Wisdom treats the number 1 as the symbol for unity. If the 1 is divided by 7 we get .142857 recurring infinitely, which brings us to consideration of the Enneagram (Greek *ennea* indicates 9 and *gram* is symbol). So it is a 9-pointed symbolic representation of the structure and movement of the Universe and has been part of the Sufi tradition for many centuries.

The symbol was, after much searching on his part, brought to the notice of the Western world by G.I. Gurdjieff early this century, and some aspects of the Sufi teachings are included in the various books setting out the methods espoused by Gurdjieff, in which the Enneagram is discussed at some length.

The Sufis have guarded their esoteric knowledge, of which the Enneagram is a part, right up to the present century, a period upwards of 4,000 years.

It is said that this symbol has a wealth of meaning and gives all the knowledge needed for an understanding of how the universe works. Note that the symbol is made up of a triangle and a hexagon. If we number the points 1 to 9 with 9 at the top, the hexagon gives the number sequence 142857. (Dividing one by seven also gives the result .142857 recurring). *So the Enneagram indicates a six-figure closed system repeating endlessly*, plus the triangle with its multiples of three which is the *symbol of the Law of Three which allows progress.*

142857 *added together* until it reduces to a single figure totals 9. (See also Appendix A for a musical model.)

The Sufis used these number patterns in their sacred dances. Dance may have been their method of keeping the Enneagram alive in memory, but I believe there may have been other reasons too, such as that the movements could result in the creation of higher energies.

If these ideas correctly interpret the Enneagram's meaning, we are faced with the intriguing possibility that the Sufis had all along possessed an understanding of chaos theory and the working of attractors.

Remembering that the closed system number is arrived at by dividing one by seven, purely speculatively it is possible to see the number one as indicative of the Creator, and the numbers three and seven as the basis of continuing creation. Point nine recurring would be the nearest that form could get to the unity of the One.

THE SUFI ENNEAGRAM AND THE VEDIC SQUARE

It is interesting to compare these two ancient mathematical systems: The Vedic Square gives a system of numbers from which symmetrical diagrams may be extracted. The Sufi Enneagram gives a diagram from which significant numbers may be extracted.

They both agree on the importance of the number 9, and how it governs all aspects of both systems with their complementary numbers.

There is worldwide evidence indicating that various peoples of the past had possessed an understanding of the solar system.

Experts who have studied ancient sites such as Stonehenge and structures like the Great Pyramids find evidence that these structures were created by people who possessed astronomical awareness and advanced mathematical knowledge.

Churches in the sixteenth century were deliberately planned according to classical musical intervals, many Gothic cathedrals corresponding to similar harmonics. I understand that the mathematics of both the music and the architecture can also be applied to the spatial geometry of the whole solar system.

It is said that the secret knowledge of the Masonic lodges included 'magic' number squares which derived from various sacred sources, including mediaeval transcendental magic, the Hebrew cabalists and the early Christian Gnostics.

There is no consensus among scientists on the importance or otherwise of a mathematically based cosmos. Physicist David Bohm and Rupert Sheldrake, whilst sharing – in their different ways – a belief in worlds other than this one, are poles apart on the subject of a numerical basis for the universe. Says Sheldrake,

> Pythagoras, of course, would wish to derive all the forms of things from some basic numerical principles or ratios, and I think there's a strong element of Pythagorean thinking underlying a lot of modern scientific thought. People feel that numbers are somehow fundamental, and that if you can have numerical ratios to explain the diversity of things, this is more satisfactory. That's an opinion I don't happen to share. I think numbers are greatly over-rated...Mathematics has been remarkably unsuccessful in dealing with biology and biological forms.

Bohm on the other hand thinks 'somewhere behind these molecules there is something still more subtle which we call mathematics, which rules all that'.

Both quotations are taken from US philosopher Renée Weber's book *Dialogues with Scientists and Sages*. She comments

> Unification is, at least in theory, the scientist's aim, embodied in the quest for simple and elegant laws. But I soon discover that there seem to be two kinds of scientists. For most scientists the search for coherent laws ends in equations. However, for the greatest scientists, equations alone are not enough to satisfy the scientists' wonder. It is to this second kind that I am drawn.
>
> For these rare minds, the equations merely tantalize and point to something else, the reality which the mathematics express, and it is this that these great minds seek. Thus, equations for people like Kepler, Galileo, Newton, Schroedinger, de Broglie, Planck, Einstein, Eddington, Jeans, Heisenberg, Bohm and others appear to be something of a code word, a disguise for their desire to display the source behind the equations. It was this that Pythagoras may have had in mind when he claimed that 'God geometrizes', and Galileo when he said that 'God's book of nature is written in the alphabet of mathematics.' Is it this that Richard Feynman is after when he writes 'To those who do not know mathematics, it is difficult to get across a real feeling as to the beauty, the deepest beauty, of nature.'

It is quite obvious, from the various ancient symbol and number systems which have survived, that religious and philosophic attitudes were in accord in giving importance to the underlying principles behind them – whatever those principles might be, and it would be a pity to dismiss them without at least making an effort to comprehend their message. Looking at the two systems I have outlined, the most striking aspect of both, as I have said, is the indication of control by the number 9. It then becomes necessary to find out how this, and other factors, apply to physical and biological systems, by examining some examples of these systems.

EXAMPLES FROM PHYSICAL SYSTEMS

Example A

In *The Matter Myth*, Paul Davies and John Gribbin discuss what they term an outstanding mystery of particle physics. They ask what causes the various subatomic particles to have one mass rather than another, and quote the example of the proton, which weighs 1,836 times that of the electron, but no one knows why. This ratio is one of many which remain mysterious. I am obviously not in a position to solve the mystery but nevertheless pleased to see that it fits into my system by totalling 9. *Dividing a ratio by all single numbers* could be a way of testing its integrity. Would it lose its 'nineness'? It is apparent from the results of the following examples that it does not.

÷	*Electron/proton ratio*	*Vedic Totals*
1	: 1836	9
2	: 918	9
3	: 612	9
4	: 459	9
5	: 367.2	9
6	: 306	9
7	: 262.2̇85714̇	1 + 2̇85714̇ – the Enneagramic remainder
8	: 229.5	9
9	: 204	6

So, with the exception of 7 and 9 *they are all unaffected* and remain *Vedic nines*. 7, as the Enneagram suggests, continues to be the maverick with the same recurring remainder. 9 stays within the creative triangle of the Enneagram, with its multiples of 3.

Example B

The second example is a really down-to-earth one – although it occurs in the ionosphere! Apparently the earth-ionosphere cavity acts as a natural resonator with a period of 1,250 seconds, causing the earth to resound every 20 minutes 50 seconds. Says the writer of this interesting fact, 'We live on a gigantic gong that booms out sixty-nine times every day.'

Examining this happening in the same way as the physics ratio seems best done by working on the annual resonance, using the astronomical tropical year.

One year	*daily resonance*		*Annual Resonances*
Mean Solar Days			
365.242194 ×	69	=	25201.711386
(Vedic total 9)			(Vedic total 9)

Dividing as before, we get:–

÷		*Vedic Totals*
1	25201.711386	9
2	12600.855693	9
3	8400.570462	9
4	6300.4278465	9
5	5040.3422772	9
6	4200.285231	9
7	3600.244483̇714285̇	7 + 7̇14285̇
8	3150.21392325	9
9	2800.190154	3

Again, with the exception of maverick 7 and creative 3, *the Vedic totals are all nines.* In addition, both the figure for the *mean solar day* and that of the *annual number of resonances* are *Vedic 9s.*

Note: The sidereal year (365.25636) and the sidereal month (27.32166) *also are Vedic 9s.*

30

Example C

This third example is important as its use leads to one of the basic physical forms – the spiral.

The Golden Section
The Greeks used this ratio (1:1.62) in architecture and sculpture, both renowned for centuries for beauty of form, and it continues to be used today by practitioners of the visual arts.

The ratio 1:1.62 *withstands division* in the same way as the two examples already given, viz. –

÷		Vedic Totals
1	1.62	9
2	.81	9
3	.54	9
4	.405	9
5	.324	9
6	.27	9
7	.23$\dot{1}$42857$\dot{}$	5 + $\dot{1}$42857$\dot{}$
8	.2025	9
9	.18	9

7 still maintaining its breakaway behaviour and 9 in this instance *staying 9*, seeming to confirm the importance of the Golden Section.

There are innumerable examples of spiral and double helix formations in nature. For instance, the florets in the centre of a daisy have a double helix with the ratio of 21:34, and a pineapple is patterned similarly, the ratio being 8:13.

To Summarize:

    The ratio of proton to electron
    The number of annual resonances of the ionosphere
    The days in a mean solar year
    The days in a sidereal year
    The days in a sidereal month
    The approximate Golden Section ratio   <u>Are All Vedic 9s</u>

THE PRINCIPLES OF NUMBER

underlying Order in Physical Systems

In view of the foregoing I wish to propose the existence of the following general principles:

1. THAT for the purpose of uncovering mathematical order, it is necessary to reduce all rational numbers to one or other of the integers by simply adding them together.

2. THAT base 10 is essential to the system, as each of the figures 1 – 9 has a role to play in the formation, maintenance and transformation of physical systems.

3. THAT the number 1, although lending itself to the maintenance of forms, is Unity and Cohesion.

4. THAT the numbers 3, 6 and 9 engender creativity.

5. THAT the maintenance of closed systems is carried out by using the numbers 1, 4, 2, 8, 5 and 7.

6. THAT the number 7 is primarily the agent for dissolution, having the power to separate unity into diversity.

The following types of numbers have been examined for their conformity to the above Principles:

Perfect Numbers	(see list) indicate unity by totalling 1 in every case (Principle 3) except the first which is 6.	*Vedic Class* All 1 – Unity
Prime Numbers	(examined up to 997) all reduce to one or other of the Maintenance group, NO Creative numbers appearing (Principle 5).	All Maintenance
Prime Pairs	When the relevant pairs of Maintenance numbers are added together, prime pairs invariably total Creative 3, 6 or 9. *Note*: When all pairs have been taken out, the majority of those left can also be paired, producing 3, 6 or 9.	All Creative
Decimal Reciprocals of the Primes	(examined from 7 to 97) invariably total Creative 9.	All 9
Amicable Numbers	(see list) Most pairs total 9. An interesting exception is the 7 + 7. One wonders if they appear in their chaotic role. Rather than meekly pairing off, could this be an *Amicable Divorce*?	All 9 except one 6 and the 7 + 7

Highly *Composite* *Numbers*	(see list) are all Creative 3, 6 or 9.	All Creative
Kaprekar *Numbers*	(see list) show an interesting alternation of 1 and 9.	All either Perfect 1 or Creative 9

As one would expect, *Transcendental* and *Irrational* numbers do not conform to the system, there being no way of reducing infinite sequences.

In some cases, it is clear why a mathematical type falls into a particular Vedic class. For instance, it would be surprising if a Perfect Number were to be other than a Vedic 1.

The overwhelming impression is one of order. The Maintenance numbers are obviously the 'work horses' of the system, whilst the Creative numbers are in command. This is clearly illustrated in the case of the Primes, as they are made up exclusively of Maintenance numbers, contrasting with Prime Pairs which are exclusively Creative.

Similar consistencies are to be found in the physical examples shown above.

LISTS OF TESTED NUMBERS AND THEIR VEDIC EQUIVALENTS

Amicable Numbers

Amicable			Vedic			
220	and	284	4 + 5	=	9
1,184	"	1,210	5 + 4	=	9
2,620	"	2,924	1 + 8	=	9
5,020	"	5,564	7 + 2	=	9
12,285	"	14,595	9 + 6	=	6
17,296	"	18,416	7 + 2	=	9
1,175,265	"	1,438,983	9 + 9	=	9
9,363,584	"	9,437,056	2 + 7	=	9
666,030,256	"	696,630,544	7 + 7	=	?

Perfect Numbers

Perfect	Vedic
28	1
496	1
8,128	1
33,550,336	1

Kaprekar Numbers

Kaprekar	Vedic
1	1
9	9
45	9
55	1
99	9
297	9
703	1
999	9
2,025	9
2,223	9
2,728	1
6,174	9
7,272	9
7,777	1
9,801	9
9,999	9
142,857	9

Highly Composite Numbers

Highly Composite	Vedic
12	3
24	6
36	9
48	3
60	6
120	3
180	9
240	6
360	9
720	9
840	3
1,260	9
1,680	6
2,520	9
5,040	9

It could be argued that approximations to infinitely long decimal expansions of numbers such as the Golden Section should not be used as examples, 1:1.62 not being the exact ratio. True, but after much thought I felt that it is too important an aspect of physical measurement to be ignored, and justification lies in the creativity of the earth itself, which, in its wisdom, has seen fit to use just such approximations in a variety of biological forms, such as the spiral shell and the fircone.

There is an old Chinese saying that nearly right is good enough. The ancient Chinese sages had a deep wisdom, so I think we can dismiss any idea of its meaning being that sloppy work will suffice. Rather, that we should accept the necessity of tolerances. They, like those in engineering, are an inevitable and essential ingredient of form in this happily imperfect world.

Dr David Burton, in his history of mathematics, addresses the infinite expansion of real numbers between 0 and 1. 'There can be confusion where decimals assume the value 9 after a certain point, e.g. 0.36999... which is the same as $0.37000... = 0.37$.' Is this a case of nearly right being good enough? If so, I am happy to tolerate his dismissal of the infinitesimal difference between 0.36999... and 0.37, relieved that mathematicians, too, have their tolerances, however minute.

Surely Plato had the right idea – that straight lines and perfect circles are possible only in his world of ideal forms, and cannot be realized physically. Nicolai Ivanovich Lobachevsky had a similar view when, in the nineteenth century, he put forward his version of hyperbolic geometry, in which all lines are curved, but the curve is so minute as not to show up until it reaches very large cosmic scales. Euclidean geometry, therefore, is not exact, but is a very close approximation to physical reality, and it would appear to be the case that infinite decimal expansions are to be expected as an inevitable consequence of this.

I am of the opinion that, esoterically, the infinitesimal difference is a vital one. I have already mentioned that the earth is imperfect so we need tolerances – a necessary state if creativity is to occur. The Creator needs no such tolerances, which makes quite logical the use of the number 1 to signify wholeness and unity, and that the nearest to perfection we on earth can reach is 0.9999999... *ad infinitum*. This is why I am unsurprised at the appearance of 9 in every area I have explored.

To conclude, it seems that the principles indicated by the Sufi Enneagram and the methods used in the Vedic Square do uncover a comprehensive and consistent mathematical system which appears also to embrace physical manifestations.

In *Critical Path*, Dr Buckminster Fuller makes an important point regarding interrelationships. Commenting on the plurality of physical laws such as the interaction of celestial bodies, he states that these laws

> could only be expressed in the purely intellectual terms of mathematics, which plurality of laws always and only related to eternal relationships existing *between* and not *in* any one of the inter-related phenomena when considered separately...*ergo*, they were all designedly interaccommodative like a train of gears.

That statement, couched in the inimitable Buck Fuller style, pinpoints the crucial part which ratios play, and it would be difficult to better his succinct and graphic analogy of the 'train of gears'.

> Propositions arrived at by purely logical means are completely empty of reality. It is very difficult to explain this feeling to anyone who is entirely without it. I maintain that cosmic religious feeling is the strongest and noblest incitement to scientific research.

Albert Einstein

3

THE ENERGIES OF EARTH

A phenomenon which is overdue for research is the art of dowsing – or divining as it is sometimes called. A large number of people make a good living dowsing for oil, water, minerals, etc. For anyone interested the most comprehensive book on the subject is *Divining* by Christopher Bird. Dowsers earn good money by being right – some with a one hundred per cent success rate. They are employed by the army, by private firms and all the utilities – electricity, gas, water. This is because divining works. The interesting thing is that dowsers are able to pinpoint exactly where the pipes belonging to a particular utility lie, even though all the other utilities have pipes adjacent to those being searched for. A dowser can train himself or herself to concentrate the mind on the desired material, ignoring all others.

It may be that this skill is more widespread than we suspect. I have no telepathic ability and get indifferent results with a pendulum, yet found water at my first attempt, and have seen an untrained person demonstrate ability to distinguish between water and metals and also to select a particular metal, successfully ignoring other metals.

Payl Clement Brown, a graduate of the Massachusetts Institute of Technology, worked for many years in electrical engineering, and later dowsed for the president of Mobil Oil. He said,

I have the definite impression that in dowsing I use my 'transmitter' to send down a mental wave which is reflected by deposits of whatever I am searching for. The answering reflection is not instantaneous, but has a few moments' time-lag. The signal seems to proceed at exactly 90 feet a minute. I haven't any idea why.

He claims no one has ever struck oil in places he has previously rejected.

What I have done is what any man can do with the right spiritual approach, and that approach is the truly scientific one.

Christopher Bird writes of an international congress in Paris where Dr Francois Peyre reported finding a checkerboard pattern of energy lines at intervals of 4 × 4 metres. These measurements were later confirmed by others, who added that the east/west intervals narrowed as they approached the poles. Manfred Curry, Director of the Medical Bioclimatic Institute in Riederau/Ammersee, came to the conclusion that an unidentified energy radiation was emitted at places where lines of the grid intersected.

Dr Zeboj Harvalik did a convincing test of dowsing accuracy when he investigated an area with two other workers. Each starting from a different corner and using white tape, they began marking out the intersecting meshes of the grid. When they met at the centre all three patterns neatly overlapped – a remarkably accurate achievement.

Guy Underwood, a dowser whose work undoubtedly deserves attention, was not a professional diviner, nor a son of the soil, but an educated man of good standing as an amateur archaeologist, which eventually led to his discovery of the art of dowsing.

He spent his working life, early in the century, as a practising solicitor and JP in Wiltshire, indulging his archaeological interest in his spare time, and became especially knowledgeable about the standing stones of Stonehenge. By the time he retired he had developed his dowsing ability to the point where he could detect concentrations of energies in the earth which were unknown to scientists. Stonehenge was found to be very rich in these energies, and he eventually gave all his time to field work at that site, and to researching old records which might give information about the religious beliefs of those who used the ancient sites. He also gave attention to the effects the energies had on animal and plant life. For example, he found that well-worn animal tracks were also energy lines.

He became increasingly skilled in distinguishing subtle differences in what he dowsed, able to detect some with the left side of his body and others with the right. By varying the strength of his hold on the dowsing rod he found various types of lines.

Eventually, he collected all this knowledge into a book *The Pattern of the Past*, in which he explained,

As my investigations led me further and further into my subject, and to the discovery that it overlapped a great many fields of specialist knowledge, I became increasingly aware that one man in one lifetime could have little hope of preparing more than an outline of the patterns to which such great importance had been attributed in days gone by. This was hardly surprising because what claimed my attention was a principle as fundamental, widespread and inexplicable as gravity, magnetism or other well identified physical laws. For a long time I was unwilling to believe that I was on to something, if not new, at least unwritten. But I delved into books and papers, and as I questioned and corresponded, I was to discover that in a great many spheres of learning the effects of the Earth Force were accepted without recognition of the Force itself.

Biologists, naturalists, archaeologists, historians, and many other practitioners had observed anomalies of growth and construction, and a worldwide code of symbols, without looking further. This I attribute to the limitations of specialization, and the fact that the whole range of knowledge is now beyond the scope of any one thinker, so that it is necessary for modern students to limit themselves to what lies within a manageable compass.

As a non-scientist he said he

could not hope to reduce the Earth Stones to a mathematical formula, and that the best way I could employ my capabilities and opportunities would be to set out as clearly as possible the manifestations of this mysterious force, and the manner in which it has been recognized in the past by Man, and in the present by vegetation and animals. I am in good company. Even when they used it and marked its presence, the priests and initiates of early days did not profess to understand geodetic phenomena.

The following summary of his findings at Stonehenge can give only a hint of the intricate knowledge which Guy Underwood achieved by his long period of dedicated research both on site and in written records. He believed that the Earth Force manifests itself in lines of discontinuity which he called *Geodetic Lines*, and which form a network on the surface of the earth. He found it to be controlled by mathematical laws, involving principally the numbers 3 and 7, in the arrangement of the lines and spirals, the lines being grouped in 3s and the spirals in 7s.

There are three types of Primary Lines, from which Secondary Lines are produced, some in a similar manner to ripples which disturb a calm lake. The three primary lines have many factors in common:

They appear   (a)   to be generated within the earth,
            (b)   to involve *Wave Motion*, perpendicular to its surface,
            (c)   to have great penetrative power,
            (d)   to form a network on the face of the earth,
            (e)   to affect plant germination,
            (f)   to be perceived and used by animals,
            (g)   to affect opposite sides of the animal body,
            (h)   to form spiral patterns.

Further, they had played a prominent, and possibly fundamental, part in the religion of many widely scattered primitive peoples.

The three types of lines are *Water Lines*, *Track Lines* and *Aquastats*.

The Water Line

The width of line varies considerably. When small it may seem to the dowser that it consists of one triad of hair lines.

41

When larger: at 3 feet each line is a triple (i.e. 9 hair lines formed by 3 triads). At 6 feet each line consists of 9 triads (i.e. 27 hair lines).

It has not been established if, and how far, the subdivisions continue, when of extreme width they can be 27 triads (81 hair lines).

The Track Line

Consists of 2 triples, the usual width being 12–24 inches. All old roads are aligned on track lines, and are followed by animals.

The Aquastat

Consists of two pairs of triads running parallel.

Patterns of Primary Lines' Courses

Winding
(normal)

Zig-Zag

Looped

Folded

They all normally maintain one general direction. They all cross at intervals diagonally. Where there are two main lines they cross each other. Where triples are involved, the outer ones cross each other while the centre one continues straight.

Two or more primary lines of the same type may run parallel and close together, greatly reducing the width of the lines. These multiple lines appear to have special religious significance, as they are often marked on sacred sites by notches or grooves on stones.

Blind Springs

Centres on which primary lines converge and from which they emerge, which causes the lines to take a spiral course. These primary spirals circle round the spring, eventually terminating upon it.

The blind spring was the esoteric 'centre' of the Old Religion, and was always the exact actual centre of the monuments. As blind springs and their spirals are found at the sites of all prehistoric monuments, without exception, it is reasonable to assume that the sites were chosen because of the springs' presence.

Underwood comments,

> One of the most remarkable and important characteristics of primary spirals is that the number of their coils is invariably governed by the number 7. This fact, coupled with the universal sanctity of the spiral symbol in the old religions, may throw light upon the peculiar significance associated with the figure.

The water line and the aquastat both produce spirals of 7 (or a multiple of 7) coils, and never any other number. Forty-nine coils (7 × 7) appears to be the limit.

He found, also, that large water line spirals expand and contract annually. Where several spirals congregate they do not interfere one with another.

He made the interesting point that primary lines and blind springs on these religious sites must be permanent, as

> the primary lines on such sites are marked by strict convention, and that from time immemorial they have remained stationary — otherwise the markings would now be inaccurate and ineffective.

Guy Underwood finished his concluding chapter by commenting,

> Though recognition of the Earth Force has been eclipsed for centuries and its practical application fallen almost completely into abeyance, now surely is the time for a revival of interest, supplemented by all the resources of modern science.

Underwood's findings on the use of the numbers 3 and 7 in the structure of the earth force gives further support to my theory of the six principles discussed in Chapter 2.

Another important parallel is between the formation of the primary lines (in particular the water line) and those of the Hénon attractor. The French astronomer, Michel Hénon, found this strange attractor whilst studying star clusters, which he plotted on computer, and the picture which emerged turned out to be a layered structure made up of fine, curved lines. As he watched the programme progress he saw more and more lines which on magnification began to blur and thicken, but the thickening always resolved into two distinct lines. Increasing magnification made both lines thicken and then the pair became two pairs and the two pairs became four, the process continuing indefinitely.

I am struck by the similarities between this attractor and the water line which Underwood described as seeming to consist of one triad of hair lines, but, when larger, proved to be three triads consisting of 9 lines. He reached a figure of nine triads (27 lines), but understandably was unable to say how far this multiplying of lines actually continued.

As you may recall, all strange attractors have a fractal quality of similarity between scales, so earth energy patterns also exhibiting a fractal aspect makes one wonder if they could be involved in the tendency towards order exhibited in antichaos.

A further aspect is the layered structure of the Hénon attractor, which is echoed in one of Underwood's patterns of primary line courses, i.e. the one he called *folded*. Folding, or layering, is a typical pattern in chaos and, as previously mentioned, is also favoured by David Bohm in his folding and unfolding implicate order.

Finally, a reminder that Underwood makes it clear that these energies are not merely on a plane, but are fully three-dimensional and extend both into and above the earth's surface, as exampled by the up and down wave motion he posits, and which, with the typical horizontal waviness of the lines, strongly suggests a spiral movement.

Forester Viktor Schauberger, subject of the book *Living Water*, was a remarkable pioneering Austrian naturalist and inventor, who, prior to the 1914/18 war, was in charge of the estate of an Austrian prince. During his years as a forester, Schauberger was a flawless and untiring observer of river flows. He watched the effortless movements of a grass snake in the water with its mixture of vertical and horizontal curves, saw the progress upstream of trout jumping a waterfall with little apparent effort. He eventually concluded that a natural watercourse which allows freedom of movement to the water, builds up an energy that flows in *the opposite direction* to the water, and gives the trout a free ride. The trout seeks out the energy flow and is sucked upward as if in a whirlwind. He noticed that weed, too, often faced upstream in spite of a strong downstream current.

One clear winter moonlit night he was observing a mountain pool formed within a rushing stream. The pool was several metres deep, but clear enough to see stones at the bottom, some of which were quite large. They were moving and colliding, as if pulled together, and then forced apart. He saw an egg-shaped stone almost the size of a man's head, act in the same way as the trout. 'In the next instant the stone was on the surface of the water, around which a circle of ice quickly formed.' Eventually all egg-shaped stones followed, leaving irregularly shaped ones at the bottom.

Schauberger later used the knowledge gained to float giant logs downstream, when all the experts had said it was impossible. On one occasion he noticed that a lake's water was beginning to move in peculiar spiral whorls which developed into a water-spout. 'Trees which had been dumped in the lake began to perform a sort of spiral dance, with ever-increasing speed.' The trees stood upright and then were sucked down to the bottom, the waterspout having reached the height of a house. He said, 'I had experienced the archetypal expansion of water, a renewal of water in the lake, without any inflow.'

He was convinced there was a close relationship between free-flowing water and the amount of energy it contained, and that this energy could be destroyed if, for instance, a river was diverted from its natural path.

Where he believed that water, in favourable conditions, could generate energy, Roy Underwood could conceivably have put it the other way round; that water is attracted to existing energy lines and that the course of a river is dictated, not merely by gravity, but by energy lines which keep water from becoming polluted, the highly energized water being able to lift and carry away detritus which 'dead' water would not have the buoyancy to achieve.

When we interfere with nature with incomplete understanding – sometimes with none – we have little idea of the chain of consequences which we initiate. On one occasion Schauberger remarked,

> We must learn to move matter, when we can, in the way electrons and protons move...and so, with relatively small amounts of energy we will be able to 'move mountains'.

Where the two men undoubtedly would have been in agreement is in the importance, in dynamical systems, of the spiral and double helix formations. Scientific support for this belief may be found in David Ash's *The Vortex*. These formations were valued also by the ancient priests who, from prehistoric times, had used the serpent symbol, which is even now familiar to many as the *Kundalini*.

According to the Tantric texts, *Kundalini* is the divine cosmic force in the body, symbolized as a coiled and sleeping serpent lying dormant in the lowest *chakra*, the nerve centre at the base of the spinal column. The latent energy has to be aroused and directed up the spine, piercing the *chakras* as it goes, and finishing at the thousand-petalled lotus in the head for the purpose of uniting with the Supreme Soul.

This beautiful allegory describes the action of yoga techniques aimed at transforming basic sexual energy into a higher form. The seven main *chakras* are the energy centres distributed throughout the body, and are supplied by a long, continuous energy line which criss-crosses the seven points, ranging from the base of the spine to the neck, the forehead, and finally the crown of the head.

The crossing lines work in very much the same way as the earth's energy lines, and the *chakras* can be compared with Roy Underwood's blind springs. The similarity in the construction of energy patterns in the two types of bodies – human and planetary – is to be expected if the earth is, in fact, a living integrated system, and this is discussed in Chapter 5.

I have concentrated in this chapter on one dowser's investigation into earth energies, but a great many others have become involved and are finding a variety of lines and patterns which cover the length and breadth of countries in many areas of the world. It now seems clear that there are major straight lines, which have been named ley lines, linking all places of power such as Stonehenge, St Michael's Mount and Cerne Abbas, to name but a few. These ley lines appear to cross water and continue in other countries.

There is, as yet, no scientific evidence of a technological kind for this widespread phenomenon, but that may be partly because of lack of interest in scientific circles, but also because there is, even today, no detecting equipment available as sensitive as the human body. I understand the training personnel of the army are well aware that certain areas on military training grounds have to be avoided because inexplicable magnetic anomalies interfere with their compasses, making them useless at these particular points.

Fountain International, which started as a healing group in Brighton a few years ago, publishes a magazine three times a year, and has developed a strong interest in energy dowsing. One of the founders, Colin Bloy, wrote, in a booklet published by Fountain, about the knowledge gained by him and those working with him on dowsing projects. He comments on differences between their findings and those of Guy Underwood:

Now I began to reflect on Underwood's results and our work, and wondered why, although we had found Underwood's spirals when we had followed out the resultant lines, instead of meandering lines, they were straight, and Underwood made no reference to such a phenomenon. Eventually we reasoned thus: if the dowsing exercise is not necessarily a neuro-electrical reaction to an external field, then there must be some process of selection by the human brain, otherwise he would pick up everything around him, and it's all happening. Somehow, if you go down a street, you can distinguish between ley lines, sewer pipes, water mains, gas mains etc. How does this happen?...What is necessary is for the dowser to have an image in his mind, a mental witness, of what he is looking for – a visualisation is a form of witness, but a visualisation hardly seems capable of resonating in a physical sense with the object or substance being sought.

Thus, in our view, the dowsing experience takes on a new dimension. It is a form of mental or psychic probe, a demonstration that dowsing is a prosthetic form of clairvoyance – a phenomenon we do not claim to understand but recognise to exist. In the case of Underwood, as he himself relates, he was testing the theory of Reginald Alexander Smith, that the sacred sites of antiquity were located in a specific way over confluences of underground water where they came together to form springs, blind and open, which manifest to the dowser as spiral forms.

One may well ask why country dowsers over the centuries have never reported strange energy lines across the countryside. In our view the rationale is as follows: Guy Underwood went looking for water and he found it. There is nothing in his published or unpublished works which indicates that he was aware of ley lines as energy paths. Here one may introduce the idea of the mental witness. His was water, and that is what he found. He could not find energies for which he had no mental concept; the concept of ley energies was not available to him. We owe it to Jon Michell ...and others, that a concept of ley energy paths became available and worth looking for. We feel that because such concepts had become available, we were able to find them.

None of this is to reduce in stature the work of Guy Underwood – quite the contrary. We had the advantage due to the work of others he did not have access to, though of course he too built on the work of others. His work remains monumental and seminal because he introduced a new concept into contemporary knowledge – a concept that he worked out alone for so many years, apparently without friends with whom he could share, discuss, compare, develop.

48

Philip and Alice Gilbert

4

COMMUNICATION WITH EARTH

INTRODUCING ALICE

Alice Gilbert was a young married woman when her son Philip was born in 1923, but the marriage did not last, and she was left to make a living for herself and her child although suffering from a tubercular lung, and was thankful that a BA degree enabled her to take on teaching and coaching jobs.

When she first started receiving telepathic messages she became friendly with Dr Graham Howe, a Harley Street psychiatrist. In his foreword to the first edition of her book *Philip in the Spheres*, published in 1952, he wrote:

> I must make it plain that Alice Gilbert has never been a patient of mine. She is not, and never has been mentally sick; she is a very normal, practical and shrewdly critical woman of more than usual intelligence.

She was largely responsible for building up the British section of the World Spiritual Council, working with such people as Sir Adrian Boult, the Imam Tufail of the mosque at Woking, Mr Justice Humphreys and Ronald Fussell, then Vice-President of the Buddhist Society. At one point she attended a WSC conference being held in Assisi, and remarked,

> On this Assisi trip, quite unsought by me, I supped with the Roman Catholic Prior, breakfasted with a practising Yogi, had

lunch with an Islamic Baroness and coffee with a Greek Sufi. As a *pièce de résistance*, whilst we were held up at the frontier, the Swiss Salvation Army came and played hymns to us.

The extensive extracts from her writings which follow are taken mostly from *Philip in the Spheres*.

Alice used an extract from *The Mysterious Universe* by Sir James Jeans as her preface, and it seems worth reminding ourselves of his view of cosmology, which is repeated here:

A few stars are known which are hardly bigger than the earth, but the majority are so large that hundreds of thousands of earths could be packed inside each and leave room to spare; here and there, we come upon a giant star large enough to contain millions of earths. And the total number of earths and stars in the Universe is probably something like the total number of grains of sand on all the sea shores of the earth.

The vast multitude of stars are wandering about in space. A few form groups which journey in company, but the majority are solitary travellers. And they travel through a Universe so spacious that it is an event of almost unimaginable rarity for a star to come across any other star...The majority are nebulae so far away that their light takes 50,000,000 years to reach us and each contains thousands of millions of stars. Such is the littleness of our home in space, measured against the total substance of the Universe.

I met Alice in the last phase of her life, when, after facing very difficult times and having to battle with adverse circumstances, she had found a haven in the home of two old and trusted friends, where she was lovingly cared for until released from her body. Philip, of course, I knew only from the extensive writings Alice had received from him after his death, and which were published in what came to be known as *The Philip Books*, and which she kindly made available to me. I found them an extremely impressive account of various aspects of post-death experience. As they are now out of print I intend to quote from them at some length, the information they contain being both interesting and spiritually important – in some ways unique.

Philip, born in 1923, was old enough, when war broke out in

51

1939 to think about training for a career at sea. He became a Merchant Navy officer and, in spite of all the dangers, came out unscathed at the end of the war, only to be killed instantly, soon afterwards, while cycling alone in the New Forest.

Philip and Alice had a very close relationship of the 'David and Jonathan' kind, and there are strong indications that they had incarnated together several times before, so it is not difficult to imagine the desperate sorrow Alice must have endured at that time. During his periods at sea they had learned to communicate telepathically with each other, which must have often allayed the natural anxiety which a mother would feel in those circumstances. For some two years before the tragic event took place, Alice had been receiving what she called a series of strange interventions by an Advanced Intelligence she had named the Unknown Teacher. She would always try to spare time to meditate during the day to train herself, as she said, 'to listen to the Silence' and then formed the habit of waking punctually at 4.00 a.m. and, after emptying her mind by an act of will, writing down the ideas which came to her from she knew not where, afterwards completing her night's sleep. Some of these Wisdom Teachings I have included later in this chapter.

By the time Philip was taken from her the rhythm had been established, and he was able, only a few days after arriving in his new environment, to contact her in the same way as did the Unknown Teacher. This telepathic linkage with both was maintained all her life, and when I saw her at Christmas time in 1980 (her last one on earth) she presented me with a handwritten copy of some recently received messages from Philip and which had never been published. In these he said,

> I wish I could return for a while and be with you as a flesh being, yet really I can do much more unhampered by it. Never, never doubt that I am a person and happy – till I look at the goings-on in Earth just now. All must be sacrificed to that just now. Man *is* worth saving – don't doubt this.

He also expressed his pleasure that she was with 'old friends of long ages'.

Philip soon realized that functioning there was very much up to the individual, and he set about 'learning the ropes' as he called it, and experimenting to find the bounds of possibility. It was not long before he was at work helping those who had 'come over' in a far from ideal state of mind, encouraging a more positive attitude, imbuing them, as far as he could, with a will to help themselves, and in studying the colour rays which, if knowledgeably applied, were of great benefit to those in need.

Apart from his very important 'rescue' work, Philip had a very busy life. In addition to keeping Alice informed in all matters connected with his activities, he was occupied studying mathematics and physics, and in exploring his environment further and further away from the earth. He soon found himself the head of a band of helpers and told Alice,

> I plan out and give them my ideas. Oh, yes, all those minor details are left to the workers to shape out, just as with you. The great unchangeable 'shape of things to come' is there, but we have to do the organizing.

One of the first things which claimed his attention – duly reported to Alice – was the mechanism of thought, and the telepathic waves by which they communicated. Here are some of his findings in that field:

> Philip: It seems that the whole cosmos, as far as we can know it, is made of thought or 'mind stuff', but the thought waves of which we now talk are more specifically individual waves which, by the exercise of a will, are drawn from the great whole, and projected like little fine spears hither and thither, crossing and criss-crossing – in fact, everywhere, innumerably. There are some which are almost automatic, which more or less drift along, as no conscious effort of will has guided them. So that all can be interfered with by 'cross-vibrations', and that is the biggest headache we have when trying to communicate. I must once again rub it in – the thought force is the source of energy, the creative dynamo. What you think strongly IS, as far as you are concerned, and, if you are powerful, to mould it into some sort of form. You can impose your thought images on other people, too.

The universe seems to consist of subtle essences mouldable by thought force, and the source of all thought force is the Creator, but we can't even begin to grasp Him yet. I can see this subtle essence with my new eyes – like finely-spun power rays, but I have not yet learnt the art of manipulating it.

It is wrong to discount inspiration emanating from our world. We over here do interfere – or inspire – though not as much as the more sentimental Spiritualists would like to believe. Benevolence and beneficence do seem to be the keynote of whatever it is that runs the universe – an impersonal benevolence, acting through unbreakable Laws, of course – but always so functioning as to lend a helping hand to those who get into a mess through suffering the inevitable consequences of breaking the Law. In one sense, all humanity is in that position, the innocent being compelled to share the common lot of man whilst in the flesh. I can see this now – why it has to be. The positive and willed reception of inspired messages is the required evolution for humanity, and should be striven for with care. But it is not easy, as you would realize if you could only see the tangle of *your* thought images – and yours are clear-cut compared with most.

A really strong 'block' of negative thinking can create a thought form which symbolizes or depicts the underlying ideas. Once created, this image 'lives' in a sense. It can move and is subject to the laws of magnetism and drawn to any forms of itself, and also can be manipulated and used by any strong, discarnate unevolved being who happens to be about. It can be possessed and used as a 'form'. But, in fact, such images, if dealt with in the right way, are only negation, and have no being in themselves, though they can be most disagreeable. Some are worse than others, of course, but the very worst rarely get to the earth plane except in such places as Buchenwald. Germany will be permeated with them for some time. Any spot where long-sustained cruelty has gone on attracts these images. Courage (fearlessness) and innate 'goodness' is the formula to get rid of them. Both qualities are necessary; one is little use without the other. It is essential to hold firmly to the idea that they have no real existence. Nothing has a real existence unless it is vitalized by and in harmony with the creative source, and not merely caused to move by entities who are misusing such creative force as they still possess. Etheric matter cannot be destroyed in the way that electricity can shrivel a physical object, but it can disintegrate, and a too powerful charge of Cosmic Force might have that effect on any lower aspect of form.

We hear, see, smell by our thoughts, as it were, direct. We are naked to every impact of thought. We see the telepathic waves like fine-spun bramble-like wire (yes, that is the 'cobweb' you and other sensitives feel sometimes on your forehead). These web-like rays have amazing properties, and can take on colour and shape according to the character of the being from whom they emanate. They form pictures or symbolic images in his mind as he stands seemingly inactive, and these images radiate outwards from him, seeming to blur and blend with those directed at him. The art is to learn to take in orderly succession. These telepathic waves are, of course, despatched by individual entities by the exercise of will and thought force, and yet it seems they are everywhere. The entity does not manufacture them. He 'tunes in' on to the required power by the act of willing it; he taps and one-points the projection outwards from himself. They are very forceful if deliberately projected. They move across the planetary arcs, uninfluenced by their in and out pull. They pay no heed to distance or space in the physical sense...

We must learn to 'pigeon-hole' the waves, to perceive in a clear-cut way unblurred, to give out, with sufficient will, a well-defined thought, or both what we take and receive will have a tincture of the thought – ours or the object's – blended with the original concept. We get that too, just as you do when you try to take our teaching. But here, as we advance, we become accustomed to the *idea* of conversation by thought; we learn to stop and listen as if to a speaking voice. Between you and me there is a chain – a thought-created chain – of telepathy woven into and permeated by an integral part of our respective make-ups, our love for each other, which, being spiritual, is a force as powerful as radio-activity. In our case this chain is strong and fairly clearly demarcated, amidst the web of images which surround us both, but, even so, they may envelop it and so obscure it from view for a flash.

The law of telepathy works exactly, it seems. There must be a certain degree of propulsion, in relation to the *frequency rate* of the agent. *Cosmic Force* is a great factor. For all functioning here – which is to achieve anything beyond merely existing unquestioningly – one has to learn to tap it by the use of a thought act of will. The ray of telepathy is of a 'quivery' nature, outspreading rather – like ripples. It is like a series of tiny hooks which, with incredible rapidity, build themselves up on to each other as the wave flows outwards from the prejecting agent. It enfolds its object, attaching itself rather as a bramble, sticks and impresses the centres of sensitivity, namely the solar plexus and the head. It has an amazing faculty of translating itself into whatever faculty is most *en rapport* with the receiver, e.g. in words, into visual images or into a smell or sensation. The link between you and me I see as a broad band of vibration along which can pass currents of emotion and thought. By certain processes this makes a sort of 'television square' on my consciousness, to which I can turn as I want, and in this square is showing a sort of replica of what you are doing, so that at any moment I can 'switch on' that part of my mind and see what you are doing.

Telepathic waves tend to spiral along. It is this spiralling motion which makes them so difficult to direct as they are easily diverted or impinged upon. If only you could realize the utterly bewildering nature of the conglomeration of those waves. Just think, every entity – either discarnate or who is at all advanced – is using them deliberately, and those who are ignorant are projecting them involuntarily from and to the Earth planet. With these waves, the more evolved the being is who is using them the easier it is; that is, if he and the receiver are on the same level. However, if one is very evolved and the other less so – for instance in Earth conditions (for the wave has to pass into less and less rapidly vibrating layers) – the propulsion rate is thereby lowered and the impact of interfering vibrations so much the greater.

Being electrically motivated, a wave is quite impersonal, and can be projected by a 'good' or 'bad' sender with equal ease. Yet, if the sender is imbued with negative thinking, the wave's propulsion rate is slower than one sent forth by a mind imbued with Light; also it tends to go sideways so that it can be distinguished by a being with sufficiently visual ability as to be able to see the wave, but this implies a degree of advancement usually far above earthdwellers. They function here so much more easily with no barrier of the flesh brain, which, though a most delicate receiving set, is designed mainly for physical sense impressions and needs to be trained and adapted to become highly and consciously receptive to the telepathic wave, though it is constantly receiving messages involuntarily. Here it is the very web of our existence; in fact we have to learn how to insulate ourselves from the bewildering impact of a myriad impressions. In the physical body its action is somewhat modified, though the basic principles are the same.

Much later, with increased knowledge, Philip added:

The thought web of earth is complicated. The far more powerful planetary arcs pass through and influence it – even, as it were, getting in its way, unless the projection of the thought comes from an adept. However, the constructive power of thought is so potent as to be the key to all problems.

At the time Alice was receiving this information from Philip she heard on the same subject from the Unknown Teacher:

If the telepathic wave becomes emotionally entangled – it is often very much so – it may not be easy to evaluate, and just now there is a great consensus of *fear*, whose formula is a big *minus*. Fear subtracts, denies, negates – its wavelengths can only be expressed in negation like a garden where bindweed, in itself seeming gentle – even graceful – twists and chokes all other plants. Seek to make your earthly vessel work accurately, and if it is tuned in on to the Inner Silence with purity and harmony, it will not make mistakes. Telepathic linkage is to be the future evolution of the race of man.

Philip: I have been studying the laws of propulsion rate of the thought web. It's clear that human electricity is a guiding factor; most laws which apply to electric light apply to thought. Electric light seems to be a basic factor of the manifestation of the Supreme Source. I've especially studied it and one very complicated method is to blend my 'me' into various masses of thought images as they rise and flow out – to be of them, sense their vitality and drive and then emerge. It's not easy to do.

Philip (discussing the noise of a plane passing through the sound barrier):

I am to tell you that the flash of intuition you had, has a basis of truth; it *is* the point of change over to our dimension, the etheric condition where what we do is reflected in reverse – a reflected projection which will have to be taken into consideration by earth students of aeronautics and supersonics. Yet to start with the simple concept of reflection – of mirror-like conditions will help in

57

calculation. For beyond the speed of sound is the frequency of Thought from Creative Forces.

Philip (8 years on):

Living in the plane of Mind gives one a detached approach, for one is deliberately creating, not reflecting; this entails a reorientation of the soul. When one first functions as creative rather than reflective, a reversal is felt in one's inner being, but how to describe it is beyond me. One seems to be in reverse.

In this renewed absorption in the Mind Sphere I also become aware of a concept of reciprocity. Nothing happens here or with you that does not tend to create a similar impact on the other. Ill will, good will, pain, joy, tend to permeate the other, for you reflect us, and we absorb and transmute you. You can see for yourself how far-reaching is the great upheaval and strife on earth just now, but if you destroy yourselves we shall continue to function, creating new stuff for old.

The Unknown Teacher:

The Laws of Being are subtle and inverted. The least is greater, for *power concentrates upon a point.** This applies to the life of the Spirit, and is the answer to the eternal query as to the wherefore of incarnation and to the how of Cosmic Law. This is the ultimate why.

The welding of earth-dwellers into unity is seemingly (so tiny is the planet in the cosmos) a matter which has only minor importance; but in truth the Universe is linked in a pattern of harmony, a vast orchestra. Throughout there is resonance, and the smallest part must blend – or shriek out of tune – and be ejected.

'Power concentrates upon a point.' This fundamentally important statement matches the traditional esoteric belief which goes

---

* Footnote by Alice: The words came to me very clearly...yet I could not grasp their meaning as to the 'point'. However, as I was talking to a mathematician (after he had read the passage) he astonished me by speaking of a new approach to geometry, called projective geometry, in which, so he said, 'the infinite plane is the inverse of the point', which would appear to be the same idea as is expressed here metaphysically.

back to the Ancient Wisdom. The Pythagoreans knew the importance of the concept when they stated their definition of space as
being 'the sum of points', and that the point is 'unity in
position'. Obviously, for the esotericists, the point is far more
important than being merely a convenient mathematical symbol.

Coming to the present time, Gleick reports on what happened
when the astronomer Michel Hénon was working mathematically
on the behaviour of star clusters. Seeking self-similarity in different scales of these clusters, he made an astonishing discovery,
which was that in such circumstances the core of a cluster would
collapse, gaining kinetic energy and seeking a state of infinite
density. This theory was difficult to imagine at the time, there
having been no previous observations of the kind, but it has now
gained acceptance under the name 'gravothermal collapse'. It
could equally well be described as power concentrating upon a
point.

Alice was curious to know what experiences were possible away
from earth conditions and Philip explained:

> Some activities are an extension of earth ones (or it might be more
> correct to say that in earth conditions they are the reflection of
> universal activities). Music, painting (colour), mathematics and so
> on can all be continued from where they are left off. There is so
> much that is fascinating to do and see, and the working of these
> great powerhouse to study, that intelligent people soon lose earthly
> preoccupations. We, the more advanced of us who have vision, see
> the reality of earth, the strong, clear and beautiful thought forms
> which, through creative energy, express in dense matter as the rate
> of vibration decreases. The magnetic currents draw similar people
> together, so, to some extent, classifying is automatically brought
> about by the Law here. I am learning to create a set of surround-
> ings for myself. Once, I made a complete and perfect car, and I
> got into it and began to drive. But it did not work at all well, for
> at once my Ego (his Higher Self) was away and beyond it. It was a
> thought creation which could only function effectively in dense
> physical conditions. It is not easy to explain how thought creation
> works. Things which are of the essence of mind, such as music and
> musical instruments, function admirably.

I get busier and busier. This is because I am speeding up my processes. I do not have to stop and think deliberately how to get to places.

He learned to raise or lower his frequencies so as to appear or disappear to less developed beings, as he willed.

It was difficult to master the knack of it, but now it is easy, a matter of will, thought and rhythm. In the case of the very 'lowest' the frequency is less than earth frequency; it is a good thing that comparatively few people gravitate there. A difficult aspect is that the repressed power in me which is dammed when I decrease my rate of vibration is buzzing in me like a thudding dynamo and I can't hold it in check for long. At first I was apt to vanish as far as the other person was concerned, which simply means that I have gone back to my real state.

We are not dependent on the sun for light – we ourselves are, to an extent, luminous in ratio with the degree of our advancement. Time is governed by rhythm – doing things at fixed intervals. This establishes itself, and can become as great a tyrant as the clock!

Having done his work with those who need help, he goes 'for a little light relief' to one of the places of instruction.

I do maths, or I listen to music and often, when doing that, I use it as a sort of funnel and go out on it into a wider space circle and increase my power so that I breathe for a while the 'air' of a further plane of existence. Music is one of the corridors for evolving upwards. Even a very unspiritual entity can, if he *comprehends* music, flash upwards for a brief period, but he can't stay there if his whole being is not in tune. If I am feeling like it, I act the fool with our band and sometimes we all go for a tour of places we know and watch the antics of our old friends.

Philip spoke about the relationship between sound and colour:

You have heard how sound can crack a glass – well, sound (resonance) can also affect the astral body and clear it and strengthen it, if properly applied. The laws which govern this process are very intricate and deeply interesting. You have already grasped the knowledge that colour and sound are two aspects of one same ray, so that if the senses are sufficiently sensitive, both impressions are felt simultaneously. This is how everything impacts here, and that is why this inner world can be so lovely. It explains what Oga meant when she said that 'the flowers sing'. It is their colour which gives out soft, gentle sound – not in words, but a sweet low murmuring, like young birds. One of the first things that strikes the newly-arrived is that constant inner background of a silence full of quivering sound vibrations emerging as colour rays. One cannot understand how it is achieved, but one senses it, and it seems part of one's own make-up, too. Yet the *silence* is the Truth. It seems to be the attribute of that source of power which we all know *is*, even if we can only apprehend in the vaguest way its Nature. From this deeply brooding, innermost-of-all silence seems to emerge the power which manifests in colour-sound rays, and in form – of which you on earth and I here are both examples. If you can enter even for a brief second this silence, which you call peace, you have touched truth. This you learn to do, and we strive here also to blend, in flashes, with the Ultimate.

In the magic which transforms the inner Silence into Form as you know it, Sound plays a great part. There are the Sounds beyond the Sound of the Spheres and can only come to you as a Silence. To me, also. Then, by intricate processes, this is transmuted into thought Sound (and this you can hear yourself when you open the inner ear and imagine), and from this into the soft liquid ripple of the little brook. That is the eternal process. If you could become consciously a part of it, you could yourself create form. In a way the artist, and especially the musician, does this, if ethically pure. The fluent purity and clarity of inspired sound is more potent in its effect on the Heart centre – helping it to balance with MIND – than any other external flow.

The Unknown Teacher:

Hear in Colour, see in Sound. This is a law a disembodied soul can follow. There is Sound – strive to perceive it, for the deep Silence must be penetrated, and at its heart is a pure Note. For Sound IS – a part of life. Hence its power, if used aright. The willed act of creation through the corridor of sound is productive of an ecstasy beyond all words. The image produced is a very lasting one for this process is of THE SOURCE ITSELF.

61

Philip:

All creative Force is magnetically attracted to its like and there are foci of music, colour continually augmented. These concepts spill over or 'solidify' into human minds. So you get your Beethoven, your Shakespeare and Michael Angelo. But this inner resonance is so powerful that to hear it could destroy the physical body, perhaps the etheric body also; even one pure in heart and mind and dedicated to LIGHT could not endure the full vibration of the SILENCE when expressed in SOUND. For us it is an armour of the spiritual body which may enable us to investigate the scintillating Cosmos of rays and power vibrations and not be destroyed. It was symbolized in fairy tales by the cloak of invisibility granted to the adventurer in the realm of magic.

Philip:

There are long periods when I deliberately train my thought force by meditation and by practising the creation of thought images. I can do the oddest things when I really set about it and this faculty is a joy to me. I astonish some folks and try to shake them out of their set environment by doing this. Sometimes I meditate on our ultimate destination, but usually I am content to leave this and carry on with my work. I realize that in some way, all aspects of form into which creative energy is constantly converting itself *are* the source. We are all, insofar as we are in alignment with Him, 'God'. We are his personality *en masse*. People like you and me are very minute specks of Him, but the very advanced people are more 'substantial' parts of Him and they administer the laws in a sense, though there seems to be certain automatic inevitability about the law in action. However, here we at least know by personal experience that there are higher strata.

Alice asked Philip if he knew how it all started – how *we* start:

It is very difficult for any of us to understand. The life-force – pure Spirit – emanates from the Source whose nature is always veiled, must express itself in form created by thought. And by expressing itself it ultimately enriches itself by the return to it of enriched form. So, by intricate processes, Spirit constantly takes on form.

The process of creating form is impersonal and automatic, brought about by the creative organs of the body. But the entry of Spirit, to create the 'average man' is a deep and involved process involving certain channels or corridors – which on earth we call by the name of stars, and also a blending and merging into the traits of the form into which it enters. There is a grand and loving simplicity about the scheme and our relation to it.

The Unknown Teacher also became aware of Alice's concern for man's progress:

You have asked how did it come about that an Ego starting from the Ultimate in the same fashion as its fellows should be 'evil'. Was it due to its being placed in less favourable circumstances at first, and if so is this fair? An impulse of pity stirred in your heart. I, your helper, cannot solve this for I am but an elder brother, not Omnipotence. Glimpses are granted me of that blazing iridescence from whose quiet heart the Universe is swayed. I am as you, a part, and the part by its very nature cannot glimpse the WHOLE. I know that dissolution is logically the final fate of a soul so imbued with evil that it has become a vacuum, yet, so infinite is the patience and the magnetic power of even the least atom of the positive, that it has never in the thousands of years of my conscious being been my lot to know of such a final individual dissolution. Yet never forget that no pity or infinity of love can prevent the working of Universal Law. Like must speed to like, and if the vacuum of the soul is incomplete it must inevitably lose its identity, for it is negation and cannot but disintegrate.

As your spirit begins to perceive the nature of the Universe, there comes upon you a sensation of unease, almost of dread. You realize its seeming impersonality. You do not sufficiently consider the strong and rapid vibration of the Forces of Harmony. Trust, integrity of purpose set the soul in harmony, and so his illusions, thought images, reflect this peace, this all-embracing benevolence. At one with this, the soul is full of joy and so need fear nothing. For peace is not merely the absence of strife but the presence of Harmony.

Philip gave a great deal of thought to the survival of the human race, though he warned against earth conceptions of man's importance.

> Man, the whole of him – astral counterpart as well – is but a speck in eternity after all. Yet we all, here as well, feel our importance in the scheme, and, in fact, we ARE important as far as we go. It is the great mass of us, as well as the great masses of other created worlds and suns, which comprise the Whole. It seems the battle must go on to banish the vacuum, or else the Law would never function. I am told that some solar systems have banished negation. Others have been overpowered and, losing the Light of the Source, have crumbled into emptiness.
>
> Man is suffering from the occult results of the evil generated by two world wars, and their effect on the minds of those who experienced them, communicating shock to children still in the womb. The task of cure will be long, but will accelerate in proportion to the number who seek positively to save our race.

The Teacher returned to the subject in 1979:

> Do not brood on the affairs of man at this moment of time, for the violence and mayhem are the efforts of dark forces to thwart a deep, though very gradual, staggering towards a dimly perceived blaze of transcendent Power from the silent centre of Being. As I have told you before, evil is the vacuum. Man is at a crisis. The forces he is mastering will either raise him to the status of the gods or blot him out entirely as a species; this is the issue. Should the latter happen, there will be protection of the souls of all Light bearers. Man will, we hope, emerge and be a credit, as the aeons pass, to your planetary system, instead of a menace as at present.

Alice began to have out-of-body experiences with Philip while asleep, helping him in his healing work, he guarding and guiding her in this new environment. On returning she quickly lost memory of those visits and had to rely on Philip's reports to know what had been happening.

> Last night you and I raised our consciousness together. Joining finger-tips, we began to vibrate more rapidly as the Chief's power flowed through us, and in a trice we were bathed in light. The

world where I live, to some extent a replica of yours, blurred into mist, and we were in a luminous plain of encircling white light with faintly outlined domes and pinnacles reaching upwards into infinity. These are the thought worlds of the advanced – the creations of minds immeasurably stronger than ours. Music seemed to be emerging from each breath of air: at one moment, it was a 'cello and we blended with it and tried to increase our power even more.

An indescribable joy was in our hearts. We seemed to be one person, yet we each perceived, heard and felt. Flecks of radiant power floated around us. But we could not stay too long, for you, tied to the earth plane, are not strong enough to breathe this air save for a brief flash.

During the period 1947–8 there came an extraordinary period of what Alice called Night Adventures. Philip took her exploring far outside the earth's etheric area and they both became shining light bodies of power, she always having to return, like Cinderella, to the physical body from which she temporarily escaped while sleeping. Towards the end of this time it was plain that Philip had begun to change. He assured her he would continue to tell her about himself as far as possible:

Yet it is less easy than at first, for I am withdrawing my consciousness from earth conditions. Mentally I am inseverably linked with you – that is, in the real life of our aspect of being. But the earthy curiosity about places and people is almost gone. Between you and me there is a strong, firmly spun web of thought. It existed before I came here, in fact before either of us came here. It was forged long ago. Now it can function when you open your mind, unchecked. You feel you are doing nothing much to achieve such a tremendous thing as communication with the discarnate. Yet it is just this willed 'doing nothing' which does the trick. It has taken you two years of thought control exercises. The reason I can get my 'me' down on paper through you is that we are so very alike mentally and idiomatically. We speak the same mental and spiritual language.

There is, for you and me, an increasing perception of speed and sound, which seems to unite at times into deep ecstasy. It is due to the increasing permeation of our forms with radiative light, which brings an even wider sense of power. In trying to describe to you my present state, I have to think of words to fit it; if you knew physics and I could put it into terms of frequencies and mathematical sequences it might be easier. I know how difficult it is to grasp your own basic lack of solidity, but it must be done before you can begin to understand. Try to cultivate this constant awareness. It is a matter of ordinary physics.

When I tune in to you now, I have a much clearer perception of the result, working from my vantage point in the Mind Sphere, where I have experienced the aura of the Masters, and then deliberately 'reduced' myself again to near perception of physical vibrations. It is as if I had myself become a very powerful microscope. If I fix my attention on your inner life I illuminate its whole. I wish I could make you realize what I look like now, for I have changed since I first began to talk to you. My body, the ME, is much less solid than before. It is more fluent (no word to express that exactly) as it gets more power impregnated as I leave earth conditions. I function in triplicate, but one of the persons is the centre and it glows very intensely. My two duplicates shine also, but not so much; they seem solid in a sense, but are merely shadows of the whole, though, by an act of thought, I can project a more powerful appearance into them. In all cases, they are fully equipped 'receiving stations' for thought and instruction, and all that they absorb impacts upon my central Self, if I so desire.

As time went on Philip learned to tap into the thought records in order to recover memory of previous incarnations, and Alice received many stories of their lives together. Philip found that the amount of recall varied in proportion to the significance of a particular incarnation. On one occasion he reported a night visit they had made together to Tibet:

It was into past scenes that we delved. We stood at dawn and watched the glow of sunrise over the peaks; we saw the heavy shouldered yaks tugging at their loads. We heard the rich resonance of the ancient gong which called us to the ancient mysteries. We were, I think, blood brothers in those days. We were monks in the inner ring and studied the mysteries, which is really only the occult knowledge you give out of the power of thought and the laws of the inevitable consequences. But we had original and independent minds – you aggressively so – and would not accept all. We set our face against intolerant practices, and were condemned to death. But it seems the Grand Lama, who also was inspired by our Master, was shown in a vision what was happening in the remote temple where we played our little part, and by the power of his thought, arrested the knife of sacrifice just as it was poised over your heart. After that, we were much respected. We became the heads of the monastery and inaugurated a new system of teaching.

One night, as Alice joined Philip for their night's adventure, Philip said, 'I want to take you to Tibet. Not the Tibet of today; we are going to travel in time, as well as space. I have discovered how to do it.'

Alice tells the story:

As he spoke, we took off into the surrounding night, like two pantomime fairies! Flying rapidly over the sea we felt the impact of an electrical storm, and though our etheric bodies were impervious to harm, yet the electricity poured through us like a blast of sirocco as we passed through a thunder cloud. We were speeding, fingertip to fingertip. The power surged through our forms and we rose in ecstasy. We approached the consciousness of the higher spheres, but, after a brief second of exquisite sensation, Philip deliberately drawing deep, slow breaths, brought us down to earth again – earth in our 'astral' sense. 'Come,' he urged, 'there is a ceremony. Come, the temple gates remain open for our coming. Look below – see the land of our ancient home, the mountain tableland of old Tibet. Does it not bring it all back to you, beloved? To me, it is my home, more so than any of the earth spots I've visited. Listen to the yellow-coloured clang of the yak bells.' Gleaming against the midnight, there stood, on a peak at the edge of an abyss, a temple. Shaped like a bell, it rose in tier after tier of carven balconies thickly inlaid with bright gold. Its tall, narrow gate was a solid mass of rubies and turquoises, and over this portal blazed a curiously wrought medallion on which were carved the words of the wisdom:– To the Three in One. 'Look at it,' I breathed. 'How exquisite and yet how familiar! I know it – I've seen it before.' 'Oh, yes,' Philip answered, 'you saw it daily for nearly the whole of a life. Or rather, not this temple, which is its astral counterpart, its pure conception, unsmirched. For this is a Tibetan temple of nearly 1,000 years ago, dedicated to our master and loved by him.' The door opened. Through the surrounding mountain tops, there resounded, as from giant horns, the deep notes of the Sacred Word. We, too, paused and uttered the Word, which pealed clarion-like into the Ultimate. There was an answering reverberation, organ-like, as of thunder rolling from peak to peak. As if at a signal, came a low sound of chanting, and advancing slowly, two by two, paced monks in coarse brown robes, woven of thick wool, with leathern cowls and rough wooden sandals curved at the toes. Onward they paced, swinging great urns from which rich and resinous incense swirled and wreathed. 'Oh, Philip, you're one of them too!' 'So are you,' he replied, pointing at me. I looked down at myself. Like Philip, my own dress had changed to a woollen smock to the knees. But on my chest, which was now the flat muscular one of a lithe middle-aged man, there hung a carved medallion, a replica of the one over the temple gate. It glowed and gave out a beam of light that played over the faces of the approaching procession which now seemed endless. 'Go on!' urged Philip, for I was still dazed, being yet tied to my earth body, and neither in one incarnation nor another. 'Take your rightful place, for in our Tibetan life you were my superior in rank and became the head of the lamasery after the master had saved your life from the knife of sacrifice. I was your twin brother and I became second in rank.' I moved forward, followed by Philip a pace or two behind, and, lifting my hands with two fingers upraised in blessing, I turned and entered the temple, followed by the chanting multitude. In front of me stood the great altar of the inner temple. There was a Buddhic figure carved by the hand of a master, with folded hands outcurved in meditation, flowing with rays of golden light. Around it burned lamps of a soft violet glow.

A great dignity seemed to overshadow me, as I stepped forward before the chanting throng, and with raised hands commanded silence. Instantly the chanting ceased and for a brief moment, silence, so pregnant as to be almost tangible, came upon us. Then, in perfect unison, there resounded from every throat, like the peal of a mighty organ, the Word. The heavens quivered and a sheet of lightning enfolded the horizon, converging into a zig-zag fork of light, playing upon the great altar. It blended and stabilized itself into a glowing, vibrating form, radiating spears of light. It was the master, the Father! The assembly bowed the head three times, with joined hands held before the chest, in salute. For, it was not our habit to grovel. He did not wish it. Upright, with hands extended palm upward, we received, in quiet ecstasy, the inflowing power from the spreading aura of the Father, directly first upon us and then relayed in a thousand glancing rays upon the vast throng of the band. And, as we contemplated, our spirits left the astral, the illusion world, far behind, and we penetrated the higher spheres, achieving union for a flash, brief in time, yet infinitely potent in result, with the Ultimate. Before us, there now advanced a small band of youthful-faced monks, bearing great censers. They wove a circle round Philip and myself as we now stepped apart from each other and, extending our hands slantwise, stood so that we formed the base of a wide triangle whose apex was the master, whereupon there came a long resonant booming of the great gong of the temple. Forked lightning shot from heaven and played upon my head, illumining my aura which expanded and shimmered, as, taking a censer from the foremost monk, I cast the contents to the four winds, so that there was a cloud of incense billowing upward forming subhuman shapes in the still air. They melted, drifted, became one.

During all this, the figure of the master remained outlined over the altar, smiled at us, and with hands outstretched in blessing. I could feel the warm glow from his fingers seep into my very heart. I had by now forgotten my everyday self. I was another person, much cleverer, it seemed, but cold and not so gay, though I still felt an inward bubble of amusement, severely repressed.

And now, those warm rays emanating from the master's finger began to blend and spiral, taking shape as a softly glowing clear-cut star of light, on which were carved out in fire the mystic letters of the THREE IN ONE. It was, I sensed, the climax of the cere-mony, the initiation point. The star glided forward, seeming to be steered by the keen piercing gaze of his eyes. It hovered above our heads as with shut eyes, and hands opened, palm upwards, we stood in ecstasy so rich, so deep, that time stood still. The star descended; it touched my forehead and then Philip's with an impact swift yet powerful. I knew I was being charged with a force I could scarcely bear. I shivered and swayed, but there flowed over me at once a surge of dynamic healing energy.

The star gleamed and danced. Power was upon us all, and after a silence the voices once more rose in a paean of chanting. Sound forms drifted upward, swirling round the master's head; he smiled again and, holding out two hands in farewell, he began to blend into the infinite deep of the midnight sky. The temple rocked and shimmered, the singing multitude of brown clad monks slowly merged into nothingness.

Philip and I stood, hand in hand, upon a mountain peak, in a silence more full than words. We paused, gazing speechless at the moonlit peaks. I felt dazed. I did not know who I was, myself of twentieth-century England, or that calm cold figure, the chief priest of the lamasery. We contemplated for a few minutes. 'Who am I?' I cried out, grasping Philip in agitation. 'Eternal!' he answered. 'Time you went back. Life in the earth sense awaits you.'

So ended Alice's account of a very impressive past life. She and Philip had many adventures, some more weird than wonderful, but all of them giving us clues as to the extraordinary variety of experience we might expect to be available to us, if we so desire, as we progress on our chosen path. See Appendix B for Alice's account of one of those adventures which is repeated, word for word, as she wrote it.

The Teacher appeared twice to Philip, once in something approaching human form, Philip afterwards describing him for Alice's benefit: 'His eyes are amazing – like piercing rapiers, but there is a wonderful, amused benevolence exuding from him.'

On the other occasion, after urging Alice to stop getting in a 'flap', he said, 'I do want you to realize what a vast field of occult knowledge you have uncovered in a few years. The Master is pleased – satisfied. I was given a short manifestation of his form. I, too, was suffering from a brief moment, not of unhappiness, but of inadequacy as I surveyed the endless work to be done. Suddenly a great star appeared at my side, so that I shook and quivered. A voice bade me renew my courage. He then said that we were fulfilling our task and to warn you not to get depressed.'

The Master also mentioned the Plan to Alice. 'I speak to you – linked as always by the band of thought with my aura – from a very far sphere, where I pursue the Plan in which you, my pupil, play your part, and he who was your son in this earth life. I watch your moral battle, but only you can slay the last enemy tying you to the emotions. Let him go, and so gain him. That is the Law. In his earth life you did it, and so now. Cease to demand comfort for yourself, for his work is so demanding that he must rest when with you.'

The Plan, which was agreed prior to their incarnation, involved the training of Alice by the Teacher in the difficult art of emptying the mind and receiving, consciously and telepathically, the ageless Wisdom. It was also intended that Philip should finish his incarnation at an early age, so that he could take on the task of informing Alice about all aspects of the after-life, to enable her to give this extraordinary teaching to a weary world in the aftermath of the tragic losses and upheavals of a world war.

Then, for Alice, something quite unexpected happened in the spring of 1948. For the previous nine months Alice had been meeting regularly with a few chosen people, and a very gifted medium – a Mrs Robins. Alice had felt the need to confer with Philip in this way to make sure what she was receiving telepathically was accurate and he was always able to reassure her about this. Mrs Robins worked in trance with the help of a discarnate young girl called Oga and so, when Philip started planning a new and extraordinary venture, he knew he had the backing of this reliable team. A very ingenious and fearless adventurer, Philip was spurred by his ambition to enlighten Alice, as far as was possible, about what he experienced whenever he raised himself from the near-earth environment. He therefore planned, with the Master's blessing and protection, a series of explorations which Alice afterwards named The Relays. Direct communication is quite impossible between a being on Philip's level in those circumstances and a soul in incarnation on earth, so it was arranged for his impressions of what was being experienced to be relayed to Alice through intermediaries. Following the first relay, during the course of his usual night message, Philip explained how it had been made possible.

'Well, darling, here I am! How did it go? Were you pleased and surprised? I told you I was hatching out something! We worked very hard. We had been, as it were, tapping the power of your circle for some time, building up a focus to use on this occasion. I showed them what to do, on the Master's instructions. It was done by a sort of chain of light, by the united wills of a number of my band. Along the chain ran the strong wave of my thought. I was in a condition far away from the earth, so you got the real thing, the power of the higher spheres. A very skilled friend manipulated the instrument, and she is a very good one, but left his thought "plate" entirely blank, as you do when you meditate, and as I telemitted the thoughts, just as they came, his thought voice uttered the words into the medium's mind in the strange muted way you heard. He was, as they said, the transformer (to lower the vibrations). My power direct would have injured the medium. I feel from your thought vibrations that I have at last made you understand and convinced of US or at least as much as you can be in the flesh – this is a great joy to me. I know that we can now carry on with our work unimpeded by so much doubt and grief on your part.'

The following series of Relays were recorded, by a stenographer who was always present when the circle met.

THE RELAYS

Relay 1: Relay of the Consciousness of a Spirit

(The transmitting entity seemed to use Philip's name as a kind of radio call signal. The whole uttered in a whisper, very powerful, lyrical and gripping.)

The Voice (addressing Alice Gilbert): Philip! Philip! I want to express for Philip! I want to express for Philip! I want to try to tell you what I experience – out – away! Sometimes I am nobody at all. Sometimes I am a star. Sometimes I am a flash of light. Sometimes I come back and I have a body like the one I used to have. I *circle round in realms of light – round and round.* I see visions. I travel through the spheres. I am free! I am again like your Philip, with a body just the same. I want to express the many phases I pass through in my freedom – how I go to realms of light where I am nobody, where I have no voice, yet I can speak. I can move, I can travel, and I can see all things. I go to the places where power dwells. I am power myself. I issue forth with my power. I go to the places where love dwells. There, amidst beneficent beings, I *am* love, I am pity. I go where they create – into the Source! I have seen new creations skimming forth – creations yet to be born in the minds of men. Imbued with this power, I too can create; I can bring forth.

I see the guardian of the planet of earth. I too can become a guardian. I go where the merciful ones dwell – those who have pity and will sacrifice. I too will sacrifice; I too have pity. I climb, I soar, I rise to the upper spheres! I descend! I am again like Philip, who dwelt for a little while on earth and loved and played for a little spell. Part of me is here, part of me is there. I am divided. I have many parts, yet all are one. Free of earth, you are immense! There is no limitation.

(Interpolation by the Voice) This is not Philip's body speaking. This is Philip's thoughts, Philip's mind, but not his speech. I speak *for* Philip. I am intense. I am full of power. (It is Philip, Philip.) I love, I am full of love. I want to reach the heights; I want to bring the heights to you! I want to delve into the cells of knowledge. I want to bring the knowledge to you! I want the love of the universe. I want to bring this love to you. Oh, I am glad, I am glad I have done this; I am glad that I can show you. I have spanned the spheres. I have touched the uppermost, but I am still *Philip.*

Wherever I go, wherever I am, I am Philip. Darling, I love you.

With Mrs Robins still in trance, the girl Oga explained what had occurred.

Oga: Now Oga will try to explain what happened. It was not Philip's personality as you knew it that he wanted to express but *himself*, the real spiritual mind. If he had touched the physical body he would have had to be the Philip you knew here. He is saying, 'Tell her I have been building up for this for some time.' It had been planned so that he could hold to the thread of his thought. He was guarded and protected so that he could succeed in conveying his thought. Many would have been afraid. They would have started out and fear would have overcome them, they would have come back – descended. But he could take it and so his whole experience has been in the unusual, the Beyond. On this evening he has tried to express the immensity of spiritual life, for one entity at least. He has tried to express hidden things. He wanted so passionately for you to understand.

Alice: Was it all really planned for Philip and me to do this before we incarnated?

Oga: Prearranged. You were shown a vision of the whole of your life with all the trouble and difficulty and you chose to do it.

Relay 2: Attempt to Penetrate the Beyond by Philip

The Voice (very urgent, intense, almost alarming to the sitters): *Avoid! Avoid! Avoid the astral! Pass by! Quickly* – away – away – I approach, I *approach* the Sun – the Sun! No, not the physical sun, the *inner sun*. The Creative – the Creative. I see form – a form evolving, giving forth, shaping, descending, linking. I see the earth with more form upon it and the two link – they are welded. They are spirit and they are material – they are *Life*! I flee away again. I skirt around. I cannot go near. There are forms, tremendous forms, guarding the heart which is *Life*. No, no, this is not 'GOD'. This is a part, a part of His force. This is creative force, but only a part. This is spirit, this is energy – it is pure – it is a part of *all life*. To drive my mind back through the spheres to earth, to carry my thoughts downward, I have beings at my side. They support and hold me. My mind is blended with their mind, for they have power – they have insight – they have wisdom. I am encased in light vibrations, delicate, scintillating. I must take on a coat of duller hue before I can descend to my place. Yet *these* will know; they will help me, for I am in their hands. I cannot dispose of the form I have built by my own will. And so, I sink away, held firmly by my friends. I may call them friends, although they are mighty in power. They have answered my desire. I was not ready – yet I willed and acted and I am safe. I passed through many cutting vibrations. They cut my spirit, for they are many, I am in the track of both earth and spirit. I feel the dual vibrations. I am glad – I am happy – I return – *Guard me*!

'The group,' Alice commented later, 'awed and breathless, wondered if he were being too bold, but that night, in his message to me, Philip reassured me that he had been given permission to attempt this penetration into the beyond by "those Beings who upheld me on the wings of their majesty", and so, though terrifying as an ordeal, there was no real danger.'

Relay 3

Express, express for Philip! Far-away – Earth is illusion! Here, here is reality. Here, here is substance. Here is light. Here is wealth, wealth of intellect of mind of those who do not wear bodies, where the physical is left behind. Here is sound, beautiful sound. Here is melody. Here we live – there, you die! Difficult to express my mind, the mind of spirit, bodiless yet alive, nothing, everything, all substance, yet you cannot hold what surrounds me.

I want to tell of beyond, beyond the intermediary state, far away in the upper places. I want to pour forth mind and spirit, the essence of you and of me to convey my dwelling place to you. Beyond human comprehension, yet understandable if you will dwell on it. Here where I am are masters and adepts linked to earth by mental bonds. They are full of power and full of the essence of knowing. They appear like spears of light rooted in spirit and transfixing earth. They are appointed in certain orbits, there to convey their knowledge. They were on earth, and they travelled far away – now their intellect comes back. I hope my message is arriving, for I feel far away – like sending a message on earth by a long-distance telephone. Earth is a shadow. Here we feel life welling up and filling our being; although we are bodiless, we are life, we are the substance – we are the seed! To convey this to you has brought into action many helpers and the thought is transmitted from one to another until it reaches the medium through whose mouth it is spoken.

There are many beings, myriads who are entirely spirit, insomuch as they have never worn physical bodies. Our world is alive with beings of pure spirit commencing with minute creatures, to the gigantic forms of power, of wisdom, of music and of various attributes that are given to earth. There are many worlds and I have travelled to an extent far afield, but I have not gathered much that I can give you through this medium. The earth has its own master, its own environment, its own spiritual spheres, and to a certain extent, its own God and God Being, but that is only part of the immensity of the whole.

My thoughts now are commencing to drift. I feel that the focal point fades.

Relay 4: (from Philip)

July 11 (One of the group, Miss B, before Mrs Robins spoke, saw a large tablet, luminous, covered with words, in some oriental script, in the air)

The Voice: Words! Words! – Words! They are me – I *am* words – I cannot hear clearly – I am where words are – written words. I *am* the written words. I do not see, I feel, I feel all that is written. I am knowledge. I see a new age, a new era out of death. I see light, soft luminous light. I enter in – it heals – it is peace. I am within the healing light, near the source which flows forth through the teeming space to earth. I see pain dispelled. I see it leave the body – a distorted ugly thing. It is dispelled by the light which plays upon it. I see the broad beam, the widest centre of healing, and in it I see a cross of golden colour, shooting forth rays, into the rose of the luminosity of the beam. I see a star – it is still healing, and I see mighty figures at each point. They are tremendous in size – I am but a tiny speck. They project their rays to the inner circle from the outermost vibrations of earth, penetrating with magnetic power the invisible which is around. From the invisible a myriad beams transform again, to bring a wholesome light into the murky atmosphere of earth.

Again I turn to the Heart. It blazes – it sends out a high sweet note. That note creates! Again I look. I see a magnetic force, drawing the distorted thought aspects of pain toward itself, taking them in, and giving forth again in purity of form. I am an on-looker. I watch. I see within my narrow vision something of the mystery of good and evil. I see it has transformed evil into good, the sick distorted vision into wholesome shape.

Again I feel I am drawn away into words – words which batter upon my spirit, upon my mind – a thunder of words! These must all be translated so that they reach the written page. It is not a library – one enters, one is writing and one *is* words. To divulge mystical secrets in words, there are friendly forms, shining figures. One approaches and enters the shining form and then, the vision comes! One is future, or past, one is a sequence of visions within the form.

Again I drift back to the light, the healing shaft and I feel I am stretched within. I breathe warmth, beauty, peace. I feel the sounds beating upon my spirit, lifting it higher and higher, and on that high, clear note, I descend, down, out of this luminous beauty, away from the thunder of words, towards the place I understand. I was away; now I must return! I drift, close enfolded by my friends.

Relay 5: (from Philip)

The Voice: Away! Away! Out – out of the dark! Come – come now away from the dark planet. In the darkness is mystery, twisted truth. It is not to be made comprehensible to man. So I leave that and come away to where there is *light*. Many paths go to the high Sun, which is the heart. I am on the path. I feel the touch of others. I must keep myself away or I shall lose my own thought. There are many within the One and they crowd across the Path that I must travel to reach the star of my dream. Again I see a form, but this time it is divine, it is a form of light and it travels by my side. I look again and there is another form – so I have two, one on each side, as I journey upwards toward the light, I hear the thoughts of others. They cut across my path. They stop me journeying on my way. Yet I hear, beyond, the high still voice, which I know is the voice which I must reach. It is urging me onwards, but this body that I wear is not fit, for it drags me down. I look to my protectors for help in this. My body is stripped from me – I have no longer a form! Yet I still *feel* as I did. But now I am nothing – nothing – all thought! My guardians swiftly move me forward through the murky denseness of thought. I, too, am a dark cloud of thought, feeling in the essence of my being which is *mind*, pain, tragedy. Gradually I feel, not the frenzied thoughts of pain, but those of love, of kindliness, of benevolence. I grow rich! I feel full, full of power and full of love. I grow in my dimension. I am now more than a thought. I am a Mind with many thoughts. I see little threads of darkness falling away from what is me. I am becoming *light*. I am becoming that which can send forth. I feel at peace. The light is dazzling but it does not dazzle me for I have no eyes to be dazzled. There is an overwhelming sense of nothing. I feel that I *know*, yet what? I do not know. Yet I am within – nothing, yet within creation.

I see the pathways which have been formed by thought through which the pilgrims must pass to reach the heart of light and rest – an intermediate state where one arrives after weary journeying. My Guardians stand beside me. They have form, for they look at me and I feel their thought enfolding me. I pass within their form and we are One united in thought. I now fade – from your mind – from your thought. I fade from you.

Relay 6: (from, so Oga said, a Being who had Never Been on Earth in a Physical Body)

The Voice (far away, ethereal and 'fluent', not like the relay from Philip): I – I – I am looking, looking at your earth. I am caught and held in the mist which surrounds the earth! I do not like this mist. I have never been in the toils of a body or garmented in flesh. I see with eyes of spirit. I am *free*. But as I come to look, I feel the dragging pull of the magnetic current which is earth. I am drawn into the whirlpool of mind, of thought. I must remember what I am, or I am lost in another mind, in another world. And so, I am drawn away beyond where there is another world which belongs to your world. It is a world of light and you who for the time being are the spirits of earth can draw it to you, obliterating the mists of memory. As I look, I see new worlds, new love, new life – all to be drawn to the earth planet. The newness is there beyond the figures of power, beyond memory; it awaits the spirit. I see through your earth. It teems with life, spiritual life, which whirls round within itself, instead of opening to what awaits it. And so, by this inward turning, calamity befalls the spirit. Beyond, there is the God body, power and love!

I look at the figures which are around your earth. They are

beautiful and terrible in their light, in their power in the rays which shoot forth from every angle of their form. They are formed in the shape of humanity because they are holding the burden of humanity, but if they were drawn away from earth to that place to which they belong, then they would have no shape or form as you know it. From their centre surges mighty Power; it goes to the transparency which is earth – there it forms into living light. It is the beat of life within the earth planet.

This is a vision granted to me to give to you. I do not know if you will understand the mystical significance of what I tell you. For it is not the figures, the guardians, who hold back the new revelations; it is the spirit of man, of earth, which turns within, instead of outwards so as to grasp the beauty, the wisdom, the love, of the gods and draw it into your planet. I go through these figures. I go into that dark. I enter the light again and I am full of power – full of wisdom. I am wisdom, for the light penetrates and builds for me a body of power, of wisdom. Within the light, I *am* all things, the light beyond which could be for you also in your darkness, if you would. But when you leave the earth planet and its environment then you may become one with the new things, with new light, new wisdom.

As I watch the whirling mass which is your earth, I know the magnitude, the marvels of which you do not know, and I feel I want to bring it to you. For new understanding is coming to your earth planet through those minds which seek outwards, and by that knowledge the new will come to take the place of the old which will be cast into the dark.

I am full of the glory of God – I am full of the glory of the power, and it is with thankfulness that I leave you!! For I have *never* been near the earth and its spirits before. I am thankful to those who are transmitting my thoughts into words which you will understand and to those who are protecting me while I float between varying depths of darkness and light to transmit to you what I can see in my mind.

You have asked for knowledge of things unseen by man, of things unheard of by man, so we are trying to paint a picture for you of invisible forces of tremendous things outside of physical understanding. We hope that you will, out of this string of words, gather some information. But remember that we are trying to show you unearthly things – beyond shape or form! Man's mind is questing, seeking, but he asks only to grasp and hold substance.

But the *truth* is *not* substance! It is not physical. So the mind must go questing, must journey for that which cannot be held but must be comprehended. And we, who are far away, yet attached, are trying, by magnetic power, to draw the thought of earth outwards and upwards.

And now my spirit is weak and faint. I recede – into the Beyond. I leave with you the thought of the great harmony of spirit, united in the *one*!

Relay 7: On Healing Spheres

The Voice (not Philip): I am – I am where all is violet, violet colour, violet rays! This is the source of healing from whence all healing comes. It is whirling – violet on the outside – rose in the centre. It is formed in a giant circle. All this colour, all this vibration is *life*, separate life, individual, many lives within this one and it is all beneficent healing life. Within the centre of the rose, there is a hollow. It goes back in the funnel, a rose-coloured funnel. You travel along this and you come to wonder, glory, something tremendous that shines with a great white light, something which is terrible yet it is lovely. From the heart of this glorious Being pulsates a ruby light, giving forth lightning rays. Those who dwell on the outside of the violet ray have not been within the rose, have not seen the centre, but as they grow in magnitude and strength, drawing ever nearer the centre which is the rose, gradually they will be drawn into the funnel of light, drawn towards the heart which rests immobile, yet is full of life, motionless yet full of motion, full of light.

This is not God. This is but one of the many powers which *are* in the beyond. It is the heart of healing, healing for the spirit, healing to make grief disappear, healing for the body.

Connected with the violet circle are myriads of beings. They have not touched the colour which is there, but they hold the magnetic rays which stream from the centre that is there, and they carry them through the many spheres to earth and its astral form, and then it is brought to those who heal in the body. Those magnetic rays are most powerful. They cannot be broken nor cast aside, for they are *life*, living, vibrating, coming from the heart. As I look from a distance upon this violet world, it is full of every shade of colour, full of figures. Yes, they have figures, shape, form, faces, of beauty. There is also great sound, high sound, continual, never ceasing. It has always been, and it seems it always will be. It is a sphere.

Again, as I journey nearer, I see there are golden rays. Here again, you have a specialized life, for here you have spiritual intellect intermingled with the violet. This means that *mind, creative mind*, is working on the healing rays so that no healing can be blind, for healing must have *eyes*, mind sense from the centre. So, if a healer is working in the body with true desire to heal, he will know, see, and do, right. That which to your standards is just 'healing' is to us, the essence of purity, the essence of life. It is of the good for there should be no sickness, no corruption.

The vibration is in continual motion, continual movement, to disperse what is bad and sick, not only in the body but in the mind of humanity. Now I have described to you a purple, golden and rose-coloured world, which I say is the world of healing. This world is high in the scale of spheres. It is outside the astral world. It is beyond in the regions of truth and wisdom. The Being who is at its heart is like unto many others, for each sphere is guided by its own Being, which in appearance is as one would visualize *God*, but each is only a part of the great source. As I talk of this *One*, I see a great central light, a figure of power and glory, and within the aura of that figure whirls the many spheres of light and colour vibrations, each with its own Being in each sphere, for all is held within the orbit of his aura. The healing vibration works at a very high frequency round the Master. The white and gold colours appear to be the most rapid.

Now, as I turn away from the realms of light, I fall into a well of darkness. I pass into the darker and darker vibration of earth until I come within the *corridor*, the nearest. Here it seems dark yet I can see, for each figure that passes by me radiates light, and as these lights flit swiftly by, I know by each of them what are their thoughts, where they are going and why they are there.

Light and dark are quickly changing before my eyes. Rays of many colours vibrate out and back, so that I am trapped in the two-way current of light vibration. The nearer I draw to earth, the more I am assailed by much sound, much noise, and cross-vibrations. I feel I have completed my journey, for I have travelled from the high places down into the darkness and turbulence of earth vibration. I have finished my journey! There are many with me who have helped to try to transmit this picture of spirit.

They await now – to take me whence I came.

81

In the winter of 1946/7, only a year or so after Philip's messages started to come through, the Master began to give Alice systematic teaching on the structure of the power which sustains all planetary systems. He began by urging Alice to,

> Feel first my peace. Take to yourself this treasure; it is with joy that I pour it upon you. Yes, we feel joy in this outpouring. We do not become cold automatons when we step ahead upon the Path. Turn, turn always to this inner strength, for it is the eternal force whose manifestations in form are our exterior universe. This force is universal: it permeates the whole. It is my lot to study, to guide its course along the channels of our planet.

THE PLANETARY SYSTEMS

Their Basic Structure

Each solar system depends upon its Sun for its life-force: the sun being a focus for one ray of life force – a dynamo, a powerhouse. Pouring upon the planets in varying proportion according to their nearness to it, and to other intricate causes, it nourishes into form the life-spirit caught up in their vibrating bodies, each having its individual response, and each, too, giving *out*, from the centre of heat and force within, a ray, component of its own essence, subtly diluted and transmuted by the solar life-force within – a living ray.

Within the system, these rays interact in an intricate pattern, piercing and penetrating the thought webs of the worlds. The interacting web of rays poured forth from each great orb, feel it and nourish their fellows: so do they set a pattern of the harmony of the Absolute. Each one takes and gives in a vivid yet silent rhythm. The interrelating force is the channel and the vessel. From it emerge all the myriad aspects of form, from the ravaging microbe to the giant elephant.

But the spirit which inhabits man is of another origin: it is the quintessence, the reflection of the Source itself, and its power is illimitable.

The tree, tall sentinel of earth, has a function. It is a receiver and a giver-out. Through its outspread leaves, as along a pole, run the rays of other planets. Through them, too, pour out many of the rays coming from earth. Not all, for in a sense each tiniest plant is a receiving station, but it is the trees who receive the most. This is another function, not at all the same process as their physical inbreathing of air to nourish themselves. It is a planetary function. Their meaning and their power is occult. The force you have sensed in the forest is very real – you have come into contact with the arteries of the power of the inner world.

There is, then, a network of interrelating, interacting arcs between the planets of any one reservoir Sun. These arcs are possessed of a seeming magic quality of expansion and refraction. They form wide corridors of space and their limits are well defined.

Through these corridors must every incarnating entity pass on its immense journey: immense only in the earth sense, for this process is a *qualitative*, not a quantitative one. Stamped and entangled it must become with certain qualities of the maze of interacting rays, and upon this was founded the science of the true astrologer.

These interacting arcs, expanding ever outwards, yet capable of infinite contraction also, are the basic structure of the planetary system – the scaffolding of this immense thought-created form. Fed, as I have told you, from their Sun, and mutually nourishing, they are the corridors of silence and, at one and the same time, the channels of incarnation and the web through whose meshes the power rays of physical growth are sieved and diluted before they are picked up by those etheric 'poles' the trees, and drawn deep into the potent womb of mother Earth.

Yet the Sun is but the focus of a greater power without: the cosmic force whose magnitude cannot be conceived in word or thought or sound. For us, the planets are our study: we bathe deliberately in their varying rays: we test and measure and investigate their many aspects and their interactions upon your mother Earth.

The Moon

Pouring then upon our Earth come these planetary rays, and some of the most easily discerned – though even they are consciously known only in their light aspect – are those which emanate from the moon. The subtlety and strange power of the moon upon earth dwellers is due to her being a thrown-off portion of the earth, which, cooling and consolidating and receiving the full impact of earth rays as well as those from others, has produced an orb, cold, 'dead' in one sense, in that it gives out no heat, yet most potently alive etherically – an orb of 'magic'. The power of the moon-ray is immense, and not yet fully explored by us. It contains a subtly diluted element which affects all it nears or shines upon. But the atmosphere of this sky-wanderer is of another quality than the one we know. The rays given out are charged with the emanations of that Force which leads to occult power.

The moon-ray is not highly impregnated with what you know as electricity, though this force is found in it to some slight degree. It has an action somewhat individual to itself: it is rotatory. It does not work well conjoined to other rays.

In considering the interrelation of these varying rays, much care must be given to their differing velocity. None travel at precisely the same speed or frequency, for each planet has a differing force of propulsion. The moon-ray is comparatively slow in speed, but very rapidly vibrating, and forming a very perfectly defined arc. Do not mistake moon-*ray* for moonbeam.

The Planets

The etheric arcs, as I have described them, are ceaseless: they function (the machinery of creation) endlessly, unbroken, with flowing rhythm. Their greatest powers, as far as Earth is concerned, lie in the Sun and moon-rays, but each planet has also its individual ray, giving out of its inner self.

All inhabited (in your sense) planets give out in a concentrated aura, the spirit of their dwellers, and I can only say to you that the ray of Earth is not, so far, wholly beneficent: there is much poison in it which affects other planet dwellers. The ray given off physically – from the make-up of your Earth – is pure, rich and health bringing, but marred by this poison: your planet is not regarded with entire favour by its fellows. The planet Mars gives out high courage and endeavour: its ray is permeated with this essence. I shall not for the moment take in detail the especial properties of each planet, because there is much that, on very broad lines, corresponds to the astrologer's findings, but much has been added by him to the known facts! The planet Venus, for example, gives out a mild, beneficent ray with aphrodisiac properties very diluted, whilst Jupiter gives out a very powerful ray charged with much electricity.

The spirit due to incarnate must, by an intricate automatic process, tune itself in onto the etheric vibrations of the planet by blending with the great arcs, and so, feeling their magnetic pull, achieves its destination. So does the soul take on form.

The web-like nature of the etheric world – intricate, seemingly involved, yet actually subject to stringent law, surrounds all things, and the planetary rays pour upon it, penetrating and vitalizing, and, motivated by the force, electric in nature, which is given out, as I have said, by the Sun. This web is life, indeed, and if torn or awry, as it can become by wrong thinking in a human being, there is then a serious flaw in his functioning.

The awful danger of tampering with atomic murder is more real that ever you realize: for the thought web – the etheric body – may be destroyed, and may be irreparable.

In the future, thought force will be so developed as to be able to use the descending and ascending etheric arcs as corridors for the passage of, perhaps, even the physical body to and from the planets. There is an undiscovered force around you which can be used for this purpose. So intricate is the cosmos that even all our calculations and tabulated results of careful study of these planetary arcs cannot yield entirely unwavering results, for there is liable to be felt, from vast systems beyond us, the impact of other rays of incalculable effect, unless we were able to trace them to their source, and this we can rarely do.

All I strive to describe to you is based on intricate scientific laws which we study and must obey – laws of vibrations and magnetic currents so complex and involved that even we, with evolved intelligence and power, can grasp only those few facets of the cosmos presented to us. For infinity cannot, as I have told you, be compressed or expanded – it *is*, eternally. Each of us who serves the powers of harmony strives to grasp and to help, in his aspect, giving out our Being into Their Wholeness – a Wholeness which is everywhere, excluding time and space values.

[Reading Alice's mind, the Master corrects her impression]

The picture conjured up in your mind of the great arcs, as you have taken my words, as bands of clear-cut light, is only partially

85

true. Certainly their sphere of influence – their pre-destined course – is demarcated; but the apparent effect is not so ribbon-like, but rather that of living prisms, ever swiftly shifting. For the quivering impact of a million rays – some within, some without, the demarcated bands – is incalculable. There is never rest.

Strive also to grasp another aspect of the universal web. For the Sun, giver of power, must also *receive*, from his planetary children. Into his mighty orbit rise rays, the pure quintessence of the planetary rays as given out from each orb. These he transmutes and gives out upon the cosmos, *as our system's contribution to the scheme*. This is the inner meaning of a phrase I have given you: 'feeds on its own functioning'. It is the endless circle, symbol of the Whole.

'The Sun behind the sun' is but a way of expressing the inpouring, infinitely potent force from the cosmic whole, of which the Sun is our powerhouse. Of this force we can know little, for it is direct expression of the Source. There can be no limitation to the eternal circle. In their factual aspect the arcs may be weighed and measured and reduced to formulae – but only so far, for they are of the measure which is beyond time, beyond form. So that you, grasping them with inner vision in no clear-cut way, elusive yet illimitably potent even in this swiftly vanishing concept, have in fact reached nearer the truth than the scientist who must limit and pin down. Yet, in considering this vast scheme to which you, my child, are a minute contributor, we must not forget that it is but an atom in eternity, and that countless other schemes and systems lie in the blue, beyond our calculation. Of these, little is known, yet we, the advanced among you, receive the teaching that there are those in our scheme, even more advanced, the Sun spirits themselves, who achieve the power to detach themselves and voyage comet-like into the ultimate.

This we do know – our own facet of the cosmos is our task and our dwelling-place – to it we must confine our attention.

Viewing this eternal outflow of power – as we do in its effects on one system – we see that there is a region of negation, of lightless void, which in a sense isolates each system, and yet seeping in and functioning with the universal positive force, causes light. Yet were it to permeate the whole, chaos would reign. Such is the eternal balance which must be held.

Earth

Earth, giving out a foul auric stench, with only a small if potent breath of pure loveliness to mitigate it, is a malefic planet from the viewpoint of some others. Her ray is very powerful, for within her is much richly teeming life-force, and this, blended with the aura, is transmuted by the planetary rays and the Sun, and forms a strange incalculable ray whose impact is dreaded by those dwellers on other planets who are enlightened enough to understand, for it may lead to madness to receive it direct. And yet this strange blend has powers peculiar to itself – they seek to harness them, to enhance the lucidity of their mental body.

Jupiter

The rays given out by each planet – those blended, as I have explained, from the arcs, have each its colours. Of them, Jupiter, that vast celestial sphere, gives out, from its great bulk, a ray predominantly green in tinge, owing to its high electrical content. This is a ray of power. It blends beneficently into the arcs, charging and stimulating. The aura of these dwellers in light, for such they are, is rich and pure. This is an advanced planet, well named from the king of the gods. The beings who dwell there are nearing the highest point of planetary evolution and are ready to become one with the Sun spirits themselves, and so to merge into the cosmos. Life is supported with ease and no thought is taken. *This is the true plan of existence*, giving and taking simultaneously in harmonious balance, and therefore immortal. Radiant of form, glowing with rich colour, vibrating in perfect unison with the Source, at infinite speed, they yet remain for the most part in utter stillness of Being, contemplating the Ultimate.

Mercury

The planet Mercury is linked from afar with Jupiter by strong rays of telepathy, and the beings – strange to your eyes, could you see them – who dwell thereon can be inspired directly by the Jovians. It is constituted of a metallic substance unknown to Earth, which gleams iridescently in the light of our Sun; and no vegetation, in our sense, grows upon it. There is also a strong ray of telepathy uniting it with Earth, so that it links the highest and the lowest, and its dwellers are forever suffering this dual impact from without. Yet, being creatures who are almost entirely intellect, they have perfected means of transmuting the poisonous ray of Earth into richness and fertility, as they know it, for they grow strange metallic objects for use in their laboratories. They are learning not to be affected by the forces of the vacuum.

Venus

This is a fertile, smiling planet, wrapped in a softly luminous pink light, which is caused by its chemical make-up. It is very warm and languorous.

Mars

We will now consider Mars, that planet which your scientists believe akin to Earth. Something of the truth they have perceived, for Mars is inhabited by a race more advanced intellectually and spiritually than man, yet not so far ahead of him as other planets. Mars is the next in advancement in order of spiritual evolution, and the shadow of the vacuum touches it directly. Its chemical constituency is strongly impregnated with reddish iron ore which reflects the Sun rays in a rather crimson glow; hence its red light as seen from here. This type of soil is very tonifying; it gives off immense vigour and combative courage. But, in general, Mars – once a warring planet, as the ancients believed – has learnt the folly of destruction. He is on the upward path and lives in peace except for private quarrels which are waged with the mind.

Saturn

In considering the planet Saturn, there are conceptions almost impossible for your imagination to set out in human language. For it is the planet of paradox, of harsh endeavour. Life there is sustained but at a cost. Those who dwell are never content till they have achieved ability to traverse the barriers of the gassy abyss and climb the illusive mountains which fill their skies, which we see as a ring. Yet this achievement brings little, for they can never return. Those who by sustained effort, vanish into the ring are, as we should call it, dead. They take on a new aspect of form and sometimes achieve seventh heaven, as has Jupiter. They have evolved. But these are comparatively few. For most, frustration and hard toil are their lot. They strain, fret and strive to retain what consciousness of the Ultimate they have achieved. Yet much tenacity of purpose is learnt. The planet is grey and unlovely. Its ray given out to others rarely brings joy.

Neptune

This is a mysterious planet; it is a watery region – a vast, seething dimly-lit ocean. The beings are of vapour-like consistency themselves, yet their minds have much strange power. With the inner Ego ever evolving through the ages, as we do, the 'good' Neptunian is a being of exquisitely balanced intuition, a creator of elusive beauty, a maker of magic worlds of phantasy. It is a planet of mystery, yet very potent in its outgivings into the system.

Uranus

Of this mystic sphere little can be said for we have no great knowledge, charged as it is with some immensely potent yet erratic electric vibrations which we believe are poured upon it from some source outside the system, receiving little warmth or magnetism from our Sun. Yet fleeting visits have shown us a sphere of mysterious beauty, of magic indescribable, of electric manifestations from strange beings who do not show in any form that we can visualize except as streaks of wildfire.

Pluto

Pluto, that is so vast, so remote, as barely to seem part of the system, is yet swayed by law and by the interacting arcs sending forth emanations strangely potent, more potent than its distance would seem to warrant. This we have investigated and come to conclusions of great import. We find that Pluto is a point of linkage, of transmutation, where our system's final essence emerges from it into the cosmos, and where we receive rays of cosmic force from the limitless fields of space without.

Upon these rays I and mine have striven to focus, in order that we might conceive their nature. They have powerful magnetism and it is possible, by blending therein, to merge into the Ultimate.

The Planetary Arcs

When contemplating these arcs, *sequence* must be considered, the rhythmic inflow and outflow in its fixed routine, never varying so that we can predict the reaction in its logical result, and the mathematician could base a progression on their formulae. These planetary arc sequences would be the key to relativity in its widest sense. Their magnetic inpull is immense etherically –that is, on spirit. Reacting on what you know as nature, yet part of the wholeness of your planet, these arcs have not yet been discovered by your scientists. They are indeed that unknown X which so eludes him – the conveyors of life which he cannot imitate. They link soul with universal spirit, but cannot be pinned down into a material formula, for they are the essence of eternity.

Rhythm is, as you know, the essence of our motivation, for it is thus that the whole system of planetary arcs waxes and wanes. The flow never ceases, but there is a surge and a slackening; a regular pulsation, not strongly marked, but certain.

It is necessary to grasp that the very creative force which you call thought is, by intricate yet exact laws, also fed and motivated by the in and out flow of the planetary arcs, and tends therefore to be influenced by the type of ray produced by the whole planet. Moreover, thought can evolve. It is built up in the *source*. Nothing can be dissociated from it.

The beings who study and guide the interplay of human whorls of personality do not control. The whole process of incarnation is subject to unalterable laws of thought – and magnetism, which is a property of thought. Until you accept that thought is electrical in nature, and acts by the same laws (but infinitely more involved and subtle) as those which apply to material electricity, you cannot grasp the workings of the planetary arcs.

THE VEILED PLANET OF MIND

What the Teacher puts in front of us conceptually, Philip personalizes, as far as his stage of progression allows, and we vicariously experience, with him, the awesome explorations recounted in the Relays. More calmly, he talks to Alice in his night messages about the implications of this stage of being:

I am in the veiled planet of the mental world, the unknown, the unexplored. It is the functioning dynamo from which the world as you know it is motivated. Really motivated and *driven* – only when the scientists grasp this, will they get anywhere. For all these

90

phases are *real* – the force you know as electricity is the offshoot, the condensation of the true electricity. It is very difficult to make it clear to you about this Mind world. It is the first clear-cut state of being which is grasped when one has succeeded in shedding Earth conditions (including post-death astral or memory world). To the questing spirit it may appear at first that he has entered chaos, a blanket of darkness shot with coloured light. But this is only because he has after his struggle to evolve out of the pre-occupations of the astral, entered into a new phase, a reality so overwhelming that his new eyes cannot bear its wholeness. For this is the world of *mind* – the creative dynamo; it is permeated with the direct rays of the Source – our aspect of cosmic power – God, if you like to call it that, but only as applied to our corner of eternity. It *exists* scientifically, and not till the scientist revises his ideas of space and time will he be anywhere near the truth.

Each of us is dual; we live in the physical and function astrally also, and are attached to the Mind planet, which is the power dynamo, by thread-like rays – like puppets in a theatre. After death, we drop the physical and function astrally in the world of created thought forms. But if we are evolved enough, we can, as it were, travel up the ray and become part of the deep mystery of *mind*, driven from pure spirit – which is the Source.

This Mind sphere is vast in time and space. It is, in fact, power in action, the spirit, the ultimate, being infinite power in quiescence, undilute. When I tried to give you my thoughts in the relay to the group, they were from a part of the sphere of Mind, showing the wondrous workings of eternity.

The transmutation of pain and evil into enriched light is actually *done* – done to those putrid thought-rays which rise and merge, by intricate processes of power infiltration. No, this is not merely symbolism. It is actually so. This hidden plane *is*. We live and breathe and think through it. Thoughts are things far more truly than the solid physical condensation of them which can decay and die. Thought images remain just as long as the power holds out. In your small way, the thought world you are building up and weaving into the tissues of the web which surrounds your physical brain, is relatively permanent and will remain when your physical brain is dust. You will have to live in the world you have built until, with the power of your *mind*, you deliberately dispel it and seek the Light.

Before the scientists can proceed to any true knowledge of the nature of man, there must be some form of photographic instrument which will register thought images and the etheric body which builds them. When that can be done, a vast mass of knowledge will emerge. It can be done. I have seen such an instrument in the thought web of a scientist here, and a most delicate an intricate apparatus will be needed. So far, no instrument has yet imitated the human eye of an ordinary person. To register thought images in the way a clairvoyant does, will need much more.

This process is constant. But we speculate here as to whether, if man does not keep the upward Path, the thought web might become too clogged to admit the rays of light. This we do not know, but we do know that other planets have become negation and have disintegrated. These sterilizing rays are *life* – creation in action. As we, by our power to tune in, become one with the Mind world, it clarifies as we recede from earth conditions. Do try to keep in mind that all this can take place *on the same spot of physical space as earth dwellers are using, and yet the earth dweller knows nothing of what is going on* in another dimension all around him.

The laws of this Mind planet are just as fixed and intricate as those which regulate the physical earth, and many are the same – especially as regards the electrical aspect. Anyone who has thoroughly grasped the working of electric currents should have a rough idea of the laws of thought rays.

In the far reaches of Mind, beyond human thought or experience, there are visions, sounds, conceptions so strange that there are no words to express them. I have seen colour rays emitting symphonic poems of sound. I have seen forms, terrible and austere, expressing pure power; I have blended with these visions and felt their essence. For I, too, am Mind, having achieved this sphere of consciousness, and so, I am one with all; there is no barrier except my own incapacity – still limited by my smallness.

What I see, what I hear, I can, by a subtle process, become – for a flash of what you know as time. This art of becoming, of really entering the thought image, is one of the essential differences between my ways of functioning and yours, and it is one of the hardest things to learn to do. The image is there; an exquisite flower, for instance. One approaches, one empties one's consciousness for a second, and one blends – and one *is* that flower, feeling its colour, its sound vibration, seeing with *its* seeing. This must be done, however, always retaining that pin-point of *me*, willed, vibrating. It is a most interesting, fascinating process.

In this way one's inner self becomes full of true knowledge. At any time I can reel off the essential qualities of other objects, if I have been of them in the way I described. It is the way of acquiring Oneness, part of the life here. Hold on to the concept of fluidity. In this lies all. It is the being able to *expand* one's inner core outwards, encompassing and blending into the object which is so very different from the consciousness of earth, which is so rigidly confined – or so it seems – because of the body. But here the motive of another is, to an extent, the forerunner of this blending.

I want you to try to grasp the Sound of this sphere – the deep notes like massed cellos, so deep that you could not register them – which issues from the point of impact where creative force draws in and repels the mass thought of Earth. For us to register it is not easy. We have to tune in and let it flow through us. My being almost faints at the impact. And all this creates etheric sound, and when I blend into that sound I can rise – in it and with it, and so expand outward. But the process is involved, for to do this I have to *become* the sound – as you do when you listen to music. And that sound has power; it can be used.

So it is that the sacred word penetrates upwards and outwards – creating, as it were, a lane through the whirling vibrations of space. [Philip's mention, here, of the sacred word refers to the *om* or *aum* which is intoned musically.]

The Mind planet is linked with all other planets and all other systems – however distant – by the planetary arcs. It is the functioning of the life force of creation. To guard the planet there are great intelligences. They stand in utmost majesty, yet there is no need for fear, for their smile is like the rippling of sunlight through a field of ripe corn. They are real beings, not symbols. But they are people, not in our sense, but in the sense of 'angel' with a job to do. Twice I have beheld that smile. He who has once seen it has gained something in his make-up which can never be lost again.

I am in the sphere where the Master's aura radiates as from a sun with outspreading rays, yet not so far outspread that I cannot, as it were, move *across* their warmth and scintillating power, blending into varying aspects of their being. To do this I must aspire into his Being as he broods upon us, his helpers, opening up my entireness so as to be one with him. And so he also, in his turn, blends upwards in the great spiral of eternity, into those immensities whose activities are beyond the universe, and yet may be minute as an electron; for size is *not* in this inner world.

There is a quality about the aura of the advanced; it is sensed and absorbed by us, his helpers; it permeates and stimulates our being, for we are in fact part of it, and of the spirit who radiates it, for we are on his wavelength. Insofar as we are tuned in to him, we receive this health-giving, life-giving flow, for he is a focus of cosmic energy which he attracts by his union with it. Yet we each have our own personal aura, in a way hard to grasp; we contribute something and give it out into the whole. Yes, your thought is right, it is the same principle as underlies the planetary ray system, as the Master described. But how this focus whorl has achieved its inner essence is impossible to say, save by the long discipline of changing form, first in the physical, then, as we advance, here also. In that change, something is built, something eternal which is one with, yet individual. And so the Master takes as well as gives. So each of us who is on the upward path and has got on a few steps, is part of the group of an advanced intelligence. It is like little stars of light to look at from outside. Yes, I have managed to do even that, for this particular little whorl which is *me* is very mobile and can go places in a rather exceptional manner – it is my job. So I have got outside and seen the vast glow which is the master, and the little silver linking chains, and the points of light which are the helpers here, and the threads leading from them into the murk which is Earth. Get that picture clear in your mind.

During his period in the Mind sphere Philip had gained a good knowledge of the destiny of humanity from those who were more skilled than he, and he stated that part of the Plan is for each being to function in integration with all, in Oneness, and yet to keep individuality 'like the many flowers of a polyanthus', all moving onward and upward in the great scheme.

Part of this progression, for the Master, was intermittent withdrawal – much as Alice, in her small way, withdrew for much needed meditation to renew her forces.

The Unknown Teacher:
Far into the outer void – which is the inner by paradox – it is my intention to blend for a while. In the remote empyrean where the scintillating of cosmic flame is the landscape, there is the Silence and the Peace, as with you. In this withdrawnness I am

in my work, which you too shall share as Eternity rolls on in the ascending spiral. Deep in the heart of the outer void the power must be tapped, and relayed to those who are my servants. For this I withdraw at times, for the thought act is infinitely great and demands *the wholeness of my being.*

FINAL WISDOM WORDS FROM THE MASTER

On Will and the Law of Being – Becoming

Wisdom counsels infinite control of Will and this is the school-house of the soul. In the far recesses of time, the temple you built represents pure Wisdom insofar as Earth can grasp it. Turn there deliberately, day and night, and so you too will contribute to the pattern of this temple, which exists eternally. Steep yourself in its midnight blue, and be at peace, even in the untoward stumbles of Earth life. Yet the detachment at the core of your life spark is itself too easy to misunderstand, for it is to be in no sense negative.

In the heart of endeavour is a point of vibration, yet becoming quiescent with power dormant, to be roused again by Will. This is the Law of Being – Becoming; the explanation of action – non-action. This is a difficult teaching, my child, to assimilate, but on it depends the functioning of all being. Action must be controlled and balanced from the root of *non-action*. To us there is no passive Nirvana. Ours is the role of action based on contemplation, the twin functioning from which comes Law.

On Form and the Eternal Task

My child, I speak to you tonight to explain the Path. You study the multiplicity of Form. Each facet has its own completion, blending into the inevitable Whole, the spear point of endeavour, which is the form of the positive, piercing negation with golden flame.

Formlessness: this is an attribute of the Source only, in its ultimate expression, from whence none who have merged therein has yet returned in form. It is beyond the peaks of silence and the sea of desire – beyond things, yet ceaselessly expressed in them.

This ultimate goal of at-one-ment can be grasped only intellectually, even by those who have left the Earth-planes and are advancing in power. At-one-ment with all being we achieve and feel in service and out-giving love, yet we too have form, and every aspect of form – however advanced, potent and fluid – implies limitation, a certain setting apart. Nor is this to be deplored. Our eternal task opens before us, and detached though we be from what you call emotion, the warm beat of love for our friends still pulses through our being: we still feel the delight of companionship.

My task is man – his evolution. To this million-age duty I devote my power. For this I seek, through the efforts of my helpers near the Earth planes, my instruments. They must be much tempered and much tested. A focus even in dense matter I must have: it is no easy role.

The light is within. It will glow ever clearer. Be at peace – my peace is upon you. It is directed from the Source. It *is* the Source. Feel it, breathe it, exude it, and you too shall be of the Source.

5

THE FUTURE OF EARTH

It is difficult to believe that anyone could remain completely unmoved by the wisdom teachings of Alice's Unknown Teacher, and the cosmic view he gives of the working of as much of the universe as his knowledge allows. Also, the very detailed accounts of Philip's experiences all add up to a formidable case for reassessment of present-day views on the kind of future we might expect to be our lot.

Anyone with an interest in scientific support for this view of cosmic life might like to read the work of David A. Ash for a detailed exposition of the physics involved, but I am not in a position to assess this work. Here, from the layman's point of view, we can ask – does it all make sense – does it 'hang together'? Obviously, for me it does, and so, too, it does for a number of people whose stature means we should consider their views very carefully. Who better to start with than the great Isaac Newton himself. I find it sad that his memory should be saddled with so many misconceptions of his views, that he is thought to be the main scientist responsible for overthrowing Creator-based philosophical theories and substituting a completely materialistic one. Nothing could be further from the truth. Sir Hermann Bondi, writing in *Let Newton Be*, defends him against the charge of prejudice and doctrinaire attitudes. The fault, he feels, is not in the Newtonian inheritance, but in others' interpretation of it. He adds, 'The roots of quantum theory are firmly in Newtonian dynamics.'

In a 1986 essay 'The Scientific Revolution', Amos Funkenstein claimed to have found, in seventeenth-century writings, not a

97

separation of science and religion, but an unprecedented fusion, and that Newton constituted an example *par excellence* of this fusion.

In the Westfall biography *Never at Rest*, there are numerous examples of Newton's own writings, making his spiritual views abundantly clear. For example:

> There exists an infinite and omnipresent spirit in which matter is moved according to mathematical laws.

Clearly, spirit, for Newton, permeated all things:

> Note that it is more probable ye aether is but a vehicle to some more active spt & ye bodys may be concreted by both together...

Newton saw the necessity for the input from the highest:

> Vegetation is nothing else but ye acting of w^t is most maturated or specificate upon that wch is less specificate or mature to make it as mature as it selfe. And in the degree of maturity nature ever rests. But so far as by vegetation such changes are wrought as cannot be done without it wee must have recourse to some further cause. And the difference is vast and fundamentall because nothing could ever yet be made without vegetation which nature useth to produce by it. ... There is therefore besides ye sensible changes wrought in ye textures of ye grosser matter a more subtile secret and noble way of working in all vegetation which makes its products distinct from all others and the immediate seat of these operations is not ye whole bulk of matter but rather an exceedingly subtile & unimaginably small portion of matter diffused through the masse wch if it were seperated there would remain but a dead & inactive earth. Miracles are really no more than anticipations of natural operations. Therefore those who believe the operations of magic to be above or against nature are mistaken because they are only derived from nature & in harmony with it.

> Extension is eternal, infinite, uncreated, uniform throughout, not in the least mobile, nor capable of inducing change of motion or change of thought in the mind; whereas body is opposite in every respect.

He believed also in the concepts of absolute space and absolute time (see *De Gravitatione*).

Westfall interprets his space concept:

> Imagine then that God chose to prevent bodies from entering a certain volume of absolute space. This hole in space ('determined quantity of extension' in Newton's words) would be tangible because inpenetrable and visible because opaque. In short it would have all the properties of a particle.

and

> With unmistakable clarity *The Vegetation of Metals* proclaims Newton's conviction that mechanical science had to be complemented by a more profound natural philosophy which probed the active principle behind particles in motion.

Westfall comments on a letter from Newton to Henry Oldenburg:

> Newton offered an interpretation of the days of creation that assumed the earth was accelerated from rest by divine force until it reached its present rate of rotation. Hence the days of creation were longer than our days.

Westfall:

> Though he used scriptural phrases such as 'the end of the world', he imposed on them a theological meaning that contrasted the world with the spirit... *Rather than a cataclysmic destruction of the physical world...*he spoke of it in terms of 'ye establishment of true religion', and 'the preaching of ye everlasting gospel to every nation & tongue & kindred & people'.

Newton even made an educated guess as to the timing of the projected earth changes, to counteract the rumours, current during his lifetime, that the end was imminent. He maintained it would not occur until well into the twenty-first century. But what really brings him into line with new age thought is his belief in a living world:

> Thus this Earth resembles a great animal, or rather inanimate vegetable, draws in aethereall breath for its daily refreshment & vital ferment, and transpires again with gross exhaltations.

And:

> This is the subtile spirit, this is Nature's universall agent, her secret fire, ye only ferment & principle of all vegetation. The material soule of all matter wch being constantly inspired from above pervades & concretes wth it into one form & then if incited by a gentle heat actuates & enlivens it...

It took a very good brain in Newton's time to encompass all the available philosophical knowledge. With the passing centuries, knowledge increased to such an extent that it just had to be split into different categories, and thus specialization was born. Being a specialist in one area inevitably meant comparative ignorance in others, learning more and more detail in smaller and smaller areas of knowledge. So the reductionist physicists were breaking down matter in their efforts to find its 'building blocks', as a child takes a watch to pieces to see how it works. Now, at last, the pendulum has swung in the direction of wholeness.

In 1937 we had the famous astronomer and mathematician, Sir James Jeans, saying in his Rede lecture, 'Mind no longer appears as an incidental intruder into the realm of matter'. And, 'The universe begins to look more like a great thought than like a great machine.'

The interesting thing to me is that so many of the greatest names in twentieth-century science, including Einstein himself, have an inner conviction that there is more to life than matter, unlike the author of the philosophical quip, who said, if I recall it correctly: 'What is Mind? It doesn't matter. What is Matter? Never mind.'

David Bohm is no worse a physicist because he is a mystic – quite the reverse, I would think – bearing in mind that his theory of implicate and explicate order bears a striking resemblance to aspects of chaos theory as well as to Philip's account of the spheres. In his book *The Emperor's New Mind* (winner of the 1990 Science Book Prize) Roger Penrose, Rouse Ball Professor of Mathematics at Oxford, comes out firmly against the idea that artificial intelligence could ever match that of man's potential. Further, he is happy to make public that his work is assisted by flashes of inspiration, and that only afterwards does he justify his 'Eureka' experiences with equations. In general, many younger scientists show signs of being far more open-minded than were their predecessors. Rupert Sheldrake's morphogenetic field, mentioned in an early chapter, might well account for these flashes of inspiration which occur to many.

If there is even only the *chance* that the ancient wisdom has truth buried in it, it is difficult to understand why scientists have not used these ideas as hypotheses. After all, their method is to think of an unproven possibility and to test it. If, in the past, they had not turned their backs on the writings of wise mystics and the ancient wisdom teachings, they might have avoided some of the dead ends which were experienced. Now, when a physics theory surfaces covering other levels of being, it would be sensible to give it a fair hearing.

As far as telepathy is concerned, parts of the Bible, together with the other religions' sacred texts which are honoured and valued by millions, must, it seems, have been received at some stage, and have maintained their value over centuries.

There are numerous examples of present-day people claiming to have received information from discarnate beings. For those who believe this to be possible, it is tempting to take such writings as 'gospel truth', but discrimination is necessary, for these informers, being at various stages of advancement, could be ill-informed. In my experience, the quality of the message is what is important, and should be weighed carefully before acceptance. We each have to use intuition to sift truth from error.

A radio programme reported in 1993 that some of the most musically sweet birdsongs had been recorded, and the recordings slowed down to a speed where the sounds could be analyzed. They were found to obey the rules of harmony and composition, and to be of a high creative standard with complex structure. Can birds, too, be fed telepathically with, in their case, patterns of sound? It seems a more likely explanation than that they are individually musically educated.

As far as Alice Gilbert's ability is concerned, it seems she was particularly able, partly because she received training from an advanced being, and partly because of her strong empathy with Philip. We all have to judge for ourselves the quality of the information.

In Alice's writings it was pointed out that telepathic waves function much less easily on earth, the relevant part of the physical brain being designed mainly for sense impressions. It does not receive these waves naturally, but needs training and adaptation. I understand that a certain level of emotional involvement is necessary for its success. These two factors would account for the inconclusive results obtained by researchers of this elusive ability.

Nevertheless, whether we are able to use telepathy or not, it is now firmly established that our thoughts affect our environment, because of our force fields. At an international conference on the Frontiers of Physics in 1977, the four theoretical physicists participating agreed that data put forward by their experimentalist colleagues showed that human mentation can affect large-scale experimentation. This occurs simply by their being there. No longer, it seems, can scientists look upon themselves as impartial observers. By being present, and by their concentrated thinking, they become a part of the experiment they are conducting; and one begins to wonder how much they influence the results. This applies, of course, to us all, not just to scientists.

It has now been scientifically accepted that there is a force field around all physical forms – animal, vegetable and mineral. During the 1960s Russian scientists Semyon and Valentina Kirlian developed a technique for taking vivid colour photographs of the energy patterns surrounding forms, but which are invisible to most people, although a substantial minority claim to see auras. Further, more recently Kirlian photographs have been taken of the twelve meridians which run the length of the human body. For centuries Chinese acupuncturists have taught that these meridians exist and are the energy lines of the body, but medical scientists denied their existence.

The energy lines which dowsers find in the earth seem likely to come into the same category as meridians of the body. Perhaps Kirlian photography should be used on them also.

The Butterfly Effect found in chaos indicates that, by our mere physical existence, we inevitably affect the world in some way or other. Things would happen differently if we were absent from it. We have power, but, like the Sorcerer's Apprentice, we have no idea what effect it might be having. Thought, though, gives us the opportunity to change things intentionally, and I mean this literally. The one thing we *can* change is our pattern of thought, which is vitally important because positive thought gives energy and negative thought causes its loss. Further, being surrounded by an energy field, as shown by Kirlian photography, we can no longer think of ourselves as completely separate units. Our energies – for better or worse – are impinging on others, and theirs on us. Also, if thought has an effect on things, there are no grounds for thinking of it as insubstantial and non-physical. There *must* be a physical element to thought. So, for those who prefer to base their concepts on the scientific method, thought turns out to be of crucial importance to our existence here and now on earth.

The idea pioneered by Isaac Newton that Earth should be regarded as a living organism, is now familiar to most people as the Gaia hypothesis, although James Lovelock, author of *Gaia*, denies the Earth's sentience. If living it be, there seems to be no logical bar to its further development. If we can accept that Philip can metamorphose into a light body, why not the Earth?

There is a theory which might go towards explaining the mechanism by which this could occur, but you would have to seek elsewhere to establish its authenticity or otherwise. I speak of a report in an American journal called *The Phoenix Liberator*. It tells of the existence of what is called a Photon Belt, Figure 5.1 (esoterically known as The Manasic Ring, from the Sanskrit

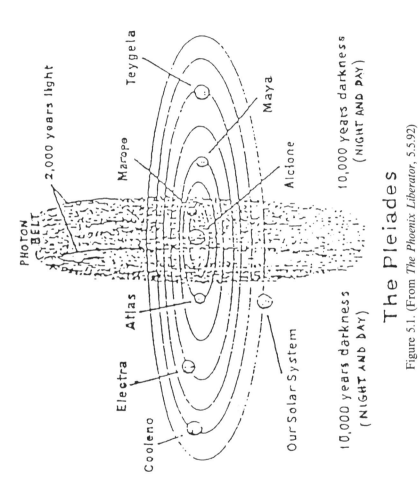

The Pleiades

Figure 5.1. (From *The Phoenix Liberator*, 5.5.92)

'manas' meaning 'mind'). It is said that this belt, band or group of light quanta encompasses the whole of the Pleiades, that group of solar systems which includes our own.

Seven solar systems, of which our Sun is furthest from the centre, revolve around a central Sun named Alcione. The light belt encircles the Pleiades at an exact right angle to all the solar systems' orbits as they follow their paths around Alcione. Our planetary system takes 24,000 years to complete an orbit, and thus we all pass through a cross-section of the light belt twice per orbit – that is, once every 12,000 years. It is a very wide band and we take 2,000 years to traverse it, during which time the photons activate all physical molecules, causing their atomic structure to change and become luminous. If this happened it would indeed be 'the end of the world' as we know it and the beginning of a new phase of existence, just as Newton foresaw.

The new phase would include a slightly diminished rotation of the Earth, causing a drop in temperature for the 2,000 years in which the Earth would be enveloped in these photons. Ice-caps are expected to extend to about latitude 40 in both hemispheres.

It seems there is geological support for this concept. Nigel Calder, in the science section of *The Guardian* newspaper (3 June 1993) reports that there is great excitement among paleoclimatologists concerning abrupt changes of temperature on the Greenland ice sheet, by five to ten degrees up, and then down. 'Such climate pulses show up in analyses of deep-lying ice recovered by drilling, and occur at intervals of a couple of thousand years or so.' He adds that no such event has occurred in the past 10,000 years, and that 'the cycles are a major natural feature of the Earth system, only recently confirmed'.

The fact that there has been no major temperature change for 10,000 years lends credence to *The Phoenix Liberator*'s claim that we are now moving very close to the Photon Belt. It is therefore a reasonable assumption that we are due for such a change in the very near future.

Thomas Khun, historian of science, in *The Structure of Scientific Revolution*, wrote:

A new paradigm or breakthrough can be achieved in science only with that kind of massive upheaval in human thought akin to earthquakes, tidal waves...as the one potentially at hand... Without really recognizing its mission as compelling human beings to question their notions of reality, physics has nevertheless spurred a quest for a new role for mind to play in the overall scheme, by continuing to open horizons broader than could have been suspected.

C.P. Snow started us thinking about the great divide between science and the arts. Now it is time to bridge the gap between science and esotericism. In the end, I believe scientists must make this leap or lose credibility in a world which is waking up, at an exponential rate, to previously unimaginable ideas.

The theme of this book has been *ongoing creativity*: in man, in nature, in the Earth itself; in the microscopic as well as in the galaxies of stars greater than we can imagine; in levels of being, seen and unseen, the unseen entirely unimaginable by humanity at our present level. But, because we are not just statically *being*, but also *becoming*, I strongly believe it will be our destiny, however many aeons it takes, not merely to imagine these things, but to experience them for ourselves.

In order to experience, we need to widen our view, to raise our expectations and to know that we each have the seed of greatness within us, but which cannot grow until we dare to aim high; high enough to join the gods as all seeds planted by the Creator may, by sustained will to progress, harmlessness to all and unconditional love.

It may take aeons for us to progress to a state of Light, and this thought tends to make the prospect seem unreal; but on the other hand it may *not* take aeons. Nature has a habit of going along smoothly for most of the time, and then, quite out of the blue, making a sudden quantum leap on to a different level of being. If the Earth should take this leap, with help from the photon belt, it is possible that the change could occur within the lifetimes of most of us living now. Remembering the fact that we are part of the Earth's environment, it is likely, in such a circumstance, that we would find ourselves participating in the sudden change, and being presented with an unprecedented opportunity to metamorphose, just as Philip did.

Whatever happens, we have a choice to make. Do we spend our time like driftwood in a stormy sea, or do we use our intuition and intellect in tandem to fashion our own surfboards, listening to all views with discrimination and accepting what is true for us? Then, if change should occur, we are prepared to ride with skill and pleasure such exciting waves as come our way, and may use the floodtide to take us to our intended shore.

EPILOGUE

A MESSAGE TO THOSE WHO HAVE READ THIS BOOK

Encountering a correspondence between two apparently unrelated manifestations is a very exciting and rewarding experience, once realized. When the idea of writing this book first came to me more than two years ago, my aim was simply to record things which had become important to me in the latter part of my life; things I had been drawn to explore and which I hoped might be of interest to others.

When I had finished writing I suffered a mystifying breakdown. I was drained of all energy and emotion, and could not function physically or mentally. I spent weeks just sitting in the sun, unable to think or read or do anything more demanding than sleep and eat. My only outing was by taxi to an osteopath who tested me with kinesiology and applied the usual adjustments, plus some medication. None of this made any difference. Three months later, when he decided to test me for poisons, up came the answer – petro-chemical poisoning. No trace was found in any of the organs tested until he came to the brain. He supplied antidotes (from Russia and China I believe), and within three weeks I was feeling much stronger, but still suffered from slow mental responses, lack of concentration and memory, all of which are still with me in varying degrees.

The manuscript having been intermittently on my mind all that time, the need to get it into print became more pressing, but at the back of my mind was the knowledge that there were correlations to be made and that I had so far not made them sufficiently explicit. One morning as I was slowly surfacing from sleep I realized I had, moments before, been experiencing that kind of correspondence very clearly, so I struggled to stay in the hypnogogic state long enough to bring that clarity to

Crop formation in the form of the 'Mandelbrot Set' at Ickleton near Cambridge. Reproduced by permission of Science Photo Library.

consciousness. I have to say that I largely failed, but a few strands have stayed with me and all I can do now is to attempt some kind of reconstruction of the clarity I had been enjoying.

Later that same day I was going through some old papers and found a letter replying to one I had sent in 1991 to Colin Andrews, founder of Circles Phenomenon Research, asking him if he thought the mysterious phenomenon had any connection with chaos theory. I had completely forgotten that he had replied saying, 'I wonder if you know that in August of 1991 a Mandelbrot Set' (probably the most beautiful and complicated strange attractor found so far, and nicknamed The Gingerbread Man) 'was formed in the wheat.' I was impressed by the coincidence of finding the letter on the day that the dream occurred.

One glimpse recalled from the dream is of strange attractor patterns which match beautifully with the shapes produced by many skilled dowsers in their search for more and more evidence of the multiplicity of energies moving throughout the Earth, not just at ground level but reaching deep down into the Earth and emerging to curve through the air also as they spiral along in all directions, making a great variety of patterns. It is worth remembering that they are not 'set in stone' but are continuously changing and developing.

A second glimpse was to do with order in simple numbers, and how this order, after translation into geometric shapes, could so easily be extrapolated into dynamic, controlled movements of the energies we now know to be the physical basis of three-dimensional life. There is agreement between dowsers' findings and the Vedic number principles. Not only that, but the dowsers' patterns fit the descriptions of strange attractors in many particulars.

The detailed description of the Hénon attractor (which I gave on page 44) and the similarly constructed water line which Underwood described in equal detail (pages 41/2) is an impressive comparison. In addition, Underwood's water line maintains similarity of pattern at all scales, giving it the fractal quality needed to qualify as a strange attractor. Are we to ignore these many similarities and pretend they do not exist because scientists have been slow to research the phenomenon of dowsing? Some may think dowsing is not a prestigious enough subject to warrant their attention, but surely it cannot be very long before the more enlightened among them change their thinking.

A similar change of attitude is to be hoped for among those who still maintain the idea of the insubstantiality of thought. I mentioned (on page 103) that thought can no longer be regarded as purely abstract as it is an accepted fact that it affects physical systems in a number of ways.

The Society of Metaphysicians has, under the leadership of Dr John J. Williamson, carried out research for over fifty years into mystical, esoteric and psychic phenomena and human abilities. The reality of these phenomena was evidenced by thought photography and later by the new and wonderful method of electro-imaging. The society provides equipment and technical guidance to many who engage in such studies, one of whom is Mrs Ruby Tonks of Heathfield. Ruby, a well-known healer and teacher in the esoteric field, was kind enough to allow me to take copies of two electro-images produced in 1995 with the cooperation of another advanced psychic, Mrs Joane Porter, who took along a pendant consisting of a silver cross encrusted with dark opals which she uses in her meditation practice. Ruby placed it on a piece of the special dielectric card used in the process, resulting in a clear-cut image with a dense energy field. A second piece of the card was put in place with the idea of attempting to produce a thought form. They both concentrated on a particular ancient Greek temple with a pillar flanking both sides of the entrance, Ruby having the difficult task of dividing her attention between the temple and the imaging process. The resulting image (page 112) shows a great deal of patterning in marked contrast to the pendant image where the surrounding area is completely clear. In the centre of the thought image is a distinctly column-like shape. Dr Williamson comments:

Our problem was to find a system which could respond to thought projections. This would give scientific evidence of the validity of most psychic processes and prove that mental energy had a real existence and effect. It would also prove that objectivity and subjectivity were relative to the location of the mind of the observer and not strictly limited to the physical world.

From early psychic photography and thoughtography our first system was photo-energy sensitive and gave clear thought pictures under suitable conditions. Later, the use of electric charges on high insulating cards and modern toners, which placed black or coloured deposits on the electric fields formed on the cards, resulted in modern electro-imaging.

Equipment and technical guidance was made available to researchers, one of whom was Mrs Tonks. Ruby showed a wonderful degree of imagination in her experiments and did not inhibit projection of the consciousness as so many more formal enquirers might do.

The pendant image shows an unusual background radiation, the fern-like images being due to particles of skin adhering to them due to handling

The thought picture, dealing with energy projection and patterning, shows random energy as well as patterned energy, the clouds and mist-like appearance being the random energies. The geode images are strange, as no contact between the card and the stones

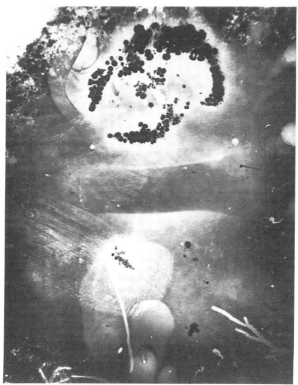

The above electro-images are reproduced by kind permission of The Society of Metaphysicians

was made. The central image of a pillar is, of course, a pure thought projection. I have many hundreds of electro-images giving a vast research field of inestimable value to future students.

Dr Williamson tells me that he would welcome enquiries from anyone interested in the society. In spite of his long and invaluable service to the society, he is still amazingly hard-working and enthusiastic.

I should like, now, to attempt to assess what contributions Alice and Philip made during a lifetime's dedicated work. If we are going to give credence to Alice at all, we may learn a great deal from her Unknown Teacher. He encouraged her (a) to feel confident of a universe based on Love, (b) to recognize an individual human's insignificance in the vastness of creation, but who, nevertheless, has a vital role to play in its progress and (c) that this progress is seriously marred by wrong action; that we cannot escape the consequences of our actions which reverberate through the universe like a never-ending echo. We have been given the gift of freedom to choose our actions, but with that freedom comes responsibility for those actions. This is not to imply that we are forced by conscience to follow a 'strait and narrow' path, but rather that good choices are available to us in abundance if we avoid negation and a downward spiral which could enclose us in ever-diminishing action stultifying progress. We are comforted by the knowledge that we are not expected to be perfect and that mistakes, honestly made, are part of the learning process.

Alice always put first things first, but I know from personal experience that she, like everyone else, had her faults. Also, in spite of the loving advice of her Teacher, she could not quite give up her grief at losing her beloved son.

The Teacher gave a great deal of information about things which were beyond the grasp of Philip, including the statement about 'the point' (page 58) which baffled Alice. She would have stood a better chance of at least partially understanding it if she had been aware of what is now common knowledge, that 'black holes' exist, and take in all available energy at a phenomenal rate. A dictionary definition describes a black hole as a region of space time from which matter and energy cannot escape. It could be a star which has collapsed in on itself to the point where its escape velocity exceeds the speed of light. One wonders where this energy is escaping *to*, or is it, as the Teacher describes, power concentrating upon a point? Like Philip reporting how 'a reversal is felt' when he reaches a higher plane, the Teacher speaks of the life of the spirit as being an inversion, 'the least is greater', which explains 'the wherefore of incarnation and the how of Cosmic Law'.

The astronomer Michel Hénon discovered that a star cluster's core may collapse, seeking a state of infinite density. He and Alice's disembodied Teacher appear to be talking the same language – an impressive performance of telepathy on Alice's part as she had no idea as to the meaning of what she was receiving.

Philip's gifts to us were twofold. He gave us the benefit of his unique experiences, and he also gave us knowledge about many aspects of our possible future environments. In giving this knowledge he is helping us to increase our power. It brings home to us the vast amount of energy there is in an idea that is followed through. When we put an idea into practice we are starting our real work in the universe. We, in our small way, are joining the ranks of the creators of the universe. Instead of reflecting, Philip said, we start to create, and when we progress far enough we are able even to create form which, as we have learnt, is achieved through thought.

For those of us who have heard, and take seriously, the New Age ideas which include the possibility of metamorphosis of the three-dimensional bodily form into a light body, instead of going through the death process and leaving the body behind, Philip's firsthand account of what it feels like to transform to a more advanced state makes fascinating reading. It is true that, in Philip's case, he did go through the normal dying process. Nevertheless, he progressed from his immediate post-death condition to a higher energy state, so the experience would have been very similar. He just had one level less to deal with, as it were. What he tells us firsthand agrees with the esoteric view that there are 'many mansions' – many levels above the three-dimensional one.

There, Philip said, the velocity of sound and the speed of light can exceed their earthly limits. He adds a third one (of which scientists are so far unaware) – the speed of thought. Each level of existence has its own wavelength; the higher the level the shorter the wavelength is and consequently the faster everything works, including the speeds of sound, light and thought. Form becomes progressively lighter in weight and matter finer and finer. As I said above, Philip experienced, at the point of entry to each level, some kind of 'reversal' which he had difficulty in analyzing and expressing, saying, 'It is felt in the inner being' – a reorientation of the soul. He *is* clear, however, that it takes place and that a reflection is received, a mirror-image (reversal again) of what is happening in the level above. As progress is made creation begins to take the place of mere reflection.

If we pause here to remind ourselves of the stretch-and-fold action which is an important aspect of chaos theory, it may throw some light on Philip's experience. The stretching and folding are not random, but are governed by strict topological laws which allow the freedom to change only within reversible limits, thus controlling the changes and keeping chaos at bay. The Lorenz attractor, formed by mapping pendulum swings in phase space, shows a structure in three dimensions appearing as a long continuous line winding from one side to the other in curves which change direction rhythmically, giving the appearance of a pair of butterfly wings. This is stretch-and-fold action of the most delicate kind in which reversals take place as the movement changes from one wing to the other in a truly creative manner, never crossing its previous path and finding an infinity of space within its finite area. Underwood's Earth energy patterns also quite literally use these rhythmic reversals.

All this brings the mind right back to Philip's experience and, of course, to David Bohm's implicate and explicate order, the theory that the very web of our existence comes explicitly into the three-dimensional world, and then folds into the implicate by reversing its action. Philip also dealt with the concept of reciprocity when he reported that 'Nothing happens here, or with you, that does not tend to create a similar impact on the other'. All types of feelings, damaging and creative alike, have their impact. 'You reflect us and we absorb and transmute you.' This important statement indicates that higher beings are able and willing to counteract, for the sake of the Earth, much of the negativity which would otherwise engulf it. One imagines that they are having their work cut out these days absorbing and transmuting!

It also means that the more we are able to open ourselves by meditation directed towards those giving this service, the better we are able to function, whatever our circumstances.

If time is taken to study the correlations between, on the one hand, chaotic and ordered behaviours observed by a variety of scientists, and, on the other, my number/geometric system and the dowsers' detailed information on Earth energies, the parallels will be found to be obvious and consistent. It may be that these comparisons were obvious to you straight away. If not, I hope that what I write now encourages you to reconsider the validity of the claims made.

Finally, I wish you a wealth of ideas, in whichever areas attract you – and may they all bear healthy fruit!

February, 1996

Commitment

Until one is committed
there is hesitancy, the chance to draw back,
always ineffectiveness.

Concerning all acts of initiative (and creation)
there is one elementary truth,
the ignorance of which kills countless ideas
and splendid plans:
that the moment one definitely commits oneself,
then Providence moves too.

All sorts of things occur to help one
that would otherwise never have occurred.
A whole stream of events issues from the decision,
raising in one's favour all manner
of unforeseen incidents and meetings
and material assistance,
which no man could have dreamt
would come his way.

I have learned a deep respect
for one of Goethe's couplets:

**'Whatever you can do, or dream you can, begin it.
Boldness has genius, power and magic in it.'**

W.N. Murray
The Scottish Himalayan Expedition 1951

APPENDIX A

MUSICAL MODEL

SHOWING HOW A CLOSED SYSTEM IS RELEASED

As shown (below) if 142857 is multiplied by any number up to six, *all the numbers turn up again in different order*. It will be noticed, also, that each of the *first sets of three* numbers has its *complement in the second set* (together totalling 999) *no matter in which order the numbers appear*, e.g.

142	714	The complementary aspect is found also, in
857	285	the Vedic Square (page 22).
999	999	

Further, the results of 1 and 6, 2 and 5, and 3 and 4 are *also complementary*, each two totalling 999,999.

DOH	× 8	1,142,856
TE	× 7	999,999
LA	× 6	857,142
SO	× 5	714,285
FA	× 4	571,428
ME	× 3	428,571
RE	× 2	285,714
DOH	× 1	142,857

The tonic sol-fa is used to illustrate the possibility of movement from a less advanced system to a more advanced one.

Multiplying by 7 breaks the closed system and inevitably produces the creative numbers 999,999, allowing a new system to begin at the upper DOH, starting a higher scale.

Notice the similarity in the numbers at the bottom and top DOH, the end 7 becoming 6, and 1 appearing at the beginning. Thus the top DOH still adds to 9, $(1+1+4+2+8+5+6=27=9)$.

118

APPENDIX B

The Story of Atlantis, received by Alice Gilbert from Philip, is a plausible eye witness account of the building of Noah's Ark, the biblical tale of the flood and the sinking of a continent known as Atlantis into what became known as the Atlantic Ocean. Alice was adamant that she knew almost nothing of the Atlantis myth at the time of writing, and was not interested in the subject. The whole story was taken down in small episodes, night after night, during the autumn and winter of 1947, and originally appeared in *Philip in the Spheres* by Alice Gilbert, published by The Aquarian Press in 1952.

THE STORY OF ATLANTIS

The final sinking of Atlantis was due to the activities of a group of wizards, who quite without realizing it, had stumbled upon atomic energy. They tapped the centres of heat and force in the inner earth and blew up a great portion of the earth's surface.

Our home was approximately where England is now, but in mid-continent. We were both male, and of the doctor fraternity, in the advanced colleges of knowledge and power.

Our first meeting was when, as two youths throwing the discus in an orchard, we fell into talk and from that day were seldom apart.

The Atlantis of our time was a fertile plain with its capital, a white-roofed city, overtopped by the golden dome of the Sun temple, at the foot of a chain of extinct volcanoes.

All inhabitants, even the poorest slave, knew something of occult power, but in the great temples, and among the elders of the city, what you know as the Ancient Wisdom was to them as the ABC.

We constantly took part in guessing games which demanded a knowledge of telepathy, in hide-and-seek which required an ability to see the aura or to psychometrize.

But in our day, there was much activity of the enemy of light. Princes, priests, the merchant classes sought for gain. The Wisdom, with the power it gave, was debased and used for private ends. Witchcraft, the casting of the 'evil eye' was a recognized means of attacking the enemy and the Venusberg, or the 'black mass' were but child's play to a night out in Atlantis!

Rumour spoke of one Elvideus as a black magician of unheard of power, who, in a hidden pit within a wood had lit on a secret which would make him master of the world.

You and I had no stomach for these activities. Within us burned, even as adolescents, a tiny spark of light, which taught us that the Wisdom must not be used for private ends, but in order to lose the Self, and so become in harmony with the creative will of Heaven. Yet we had much curiosity as to Elvideus' secret and sought means to discover it.

One morning, whilst still mere youths, we were playfully wrestling as we walked along between the magnolias and azaleas lining the highroad to the city, when we saw approaching a tall and powerful figure bearing a strangely forked wand.

You displayed some signs of alarm, whispering: 'It is the great prophet Noasa! I believe he is benevolent, but one never knows – best to avoid him!'

But as we made to turn off into the golden mimosa copses fringing the roadway, the prophet stayed us with uplifted hand. Eyes, deep, glowing but kindly, held us transfixed and in a mellow, resonant voce, he spoke:

'Andama and Persamen – hear my words! You are of my band: the seal is upon you! We work on the Ray of the Master. Await the day, study, gain knowledge, and then seek me. So and so only shall you escape doom. Think on my words!'

Raising his hand in blessing, he passed on his way, leaving behind him a scent as of sandalwood and roses.

We stood amazed and somewhat overwhelmed, but being young and gay, the ringing impact of his words faded into the background of memory, as we plunged into the varied activities of an Atlantean neophyte of good family and many moons passed before, once again, Fate spoke clearly in our ears.

One evening walking together upon the hills at sundown, we perceived a tree all aglow and thought at first it was some effect of the sunset. But as we drew nearer, we saw that this was no earthly light, for it was a flaming violet out of which stabbed white rays of power and we fell upon our knees, hiding our faces.

Gradually the light took form, and the form solidified: it was a man of dignity and benevolence, smiling with a gleam of amusement in his piercing eyes. We bowed to the ground, and so doing, seemed to perceive a Voice: the impact was mental rather than on the physical ear.

'You are my servants,' he addressed us. 'Do not forget this. Your part must be played according to the plan. Follow not the desires of your hearts, but the inner voice of the soul: it is from Me.

'Seek out *Noasa*, before the hour strikes! Leave all! Go! When the time is ripe: this you will know. The Law of the Inevitable Consequence must be obeyed! Not I nor any other can hold back its working, here or elsewhere!'

A rainbow-coloured fountain of light played around the form as it melted away, and a great silence was upon us both. A silence full of rich inner sound.

Uplifted into ecstasy, we brooded there till the birds ceased to chirp and twitter, and night enfolded us in its dark velvet curtain.

Returning to our homes, we meditated, each of us, turning over in his mind the strange words of the Unknown.

We had not wed. Our families, your father, a strong-willed elder of the great temple, with whom you frequently disputed, and my grandfather – for my parents had died when I was a young child – constantly set before us the names of suitable young girls so that we might enter upon the rather complicated family negotiations preceding a union, which were required in Atlantis, where a marriage was taken very seriously.

Temporary affairs of a semi-official nature were not frowned upon. There was in fact a class of women like Aspasia of Ancient Greece, whose charm, intelligence and dignity were unsurpassed, and who held a rather vaguely defined but not unrespected place in the community, and whose lives were given up to this purpose. They were not prostitutes – who were invariably of the slave-class – and these unofficial unions must last at least a year. They were not despised and indeed they were encouraged to place their children in the service of the temples.

But marriage was a solemn rite and festival, and the breaking of its bonds was regarded as a violation and a sin against the gods.

Neither you nor I would enter upon it. We had our unions, but so great was our affection for each other, based on the spirit and not on any physical aberration, that little else mattered: we had not learned, in that incarnation, to function in separation.

We determined to seek out Noasa as we had been commanded, but his dwelling was far from our city and could involve a six days' journey across the great plain and to this end, we began to make our plans.

In the meanwhile, we continued to develop our thought force. You specialized in telepathy itself and I in astral travelling. I learned to project my etheric body in the daytime, consciously, and to remember what I had seen. By long and concentrated practice we now developed this ability to project at will an 'extension' of our personality into other scenes, and to bring back clear memories.

We were now in our early thirties, at the zenith of our strength and power, and we determined, before seeking out Noasa, to use our knowledge in a supreme act of concentration, to make the attempt to penetrate the secret of Elvideus the magician, whose ill-fame increased with the passing of the years.

In order to prepare for this adventure, we retired for a while to the mountains, for this was always done when it was desired to concentrate and achieve fresh power and inspiration.

We had decided that I should be the one to adventure forth, and you should strive to rescue or bring support to me, in need.

I detached my etheric body, and you sat guarding my form which lay inert upon the couch with its sheepskin rug and monkey skin pillows. In your hands you held a parchment scroll and a fine-pointed quill, and by your side was a vase of deep blue dye and just as you do now, you opened your mind and prepared to write any telepathic messages I might project.

Giving a last glance at my form, I floated out through the closed door and down over the housetops of the city. I did not know enough merely to think myself to the spot I sought. In a few seconds, I was standing outside the great bronze gates, in the heart of a deep, dark wood, which guarded Elvideus' retreat.

Outside, there was the still and sombre power of the great oaks and beeches. Inside – the secret.

Calling with all my strength on the Unknown for help, I glided through the gates and sensed the curious impact of a strange force with which they seemed to be charged.

Pausing awhile, I took my bearings. All was quiet. It was the midnight hour, which formed a part of the very few hours of rest granted to the wretched slaves who toiled day and night to perform the magician's will. Indeed, it was for that reason that I had chosen this hour to come in this manner. For to come in the day-time, disguised as a slave would have been useless as the magician would have at once recognized me by my aura. Coming in my etheric body at a time when I might hope that Elvideus himself would be asleep and travelling in the astral, I hoped to achieve my object, undiscovered.

A lightly built fence of criss-cross slats of bronze was all the protection I could see, stretching on either side the gates and forming an enormous enclosure shaped like a five-pointed star, in whose centre gaped a deep wide pit. As I examined the fence, I saw, some steps away, three haggard, half-starved slaves, their backs furrowed with ancient weals, seemingly asleep upon their feet, holding the topmost slats for support. I drew near. Three moaning etheric bodies fell pleading at my feet, entirely severed from their forms, the etheric chord broken and decaying.

'Help us, O Shining One,' they groaned. 'We are in a fog of fear and doubt. We sought to escape, and gripped the fence to climb it and our hands were held as in a vice. Detach our hands, of your mercy!'

'Await me here!' I cried. 'And I will take you to One who will help you to learn the true life of the Spirit. You shall see light and emerge from the black grief which overshadows you!'

Turning away, I approached my real objective, the pit. About a quarter of a mile in diameter, its dark innards vanished into the deep.

A cage and a powerful pulley showed the way of descent for those in the flesh, but I, uttering a potent invocation, plunged downwards as I was!

Darkness, as you know, does not affect the etheric body whose glow provides its own light, but I was aware that there were at intervals, lamps of very brilliant light such as was not known in Atlantis.

When I alighted on the floor of the pit, another great gate confronted me, and I sensed that it too was very strongly charged with that mysterious force which had gripped and slain the slaves. Elvideus was taking no chances on any stray explorer penetrating his secret world.

I passed through the gate and along a corridor. At the end was a chamber walled in bronze and within it – the mystery! A terrible monster of pulleys, rods and shafts, uttering a deep and awful hum. Great poles rose from it and out of them zig-zagged arrows of lightning-like flame.

At this point, I paused, and deliberately telemitted to you all that I saw, as we had arranged, so that I might compare it with my remembered vision. For well I knew that memory might elude me, on return.

As I gazed, I was astonished and annoyed to see the astral form of Elvideus glide over his machine. I feared that some inner intuition had warned him of my presence, for he hovered aimlessly, and yet with a certain menace, over the retorts with their strange egg-shaped containers.

Suddenly he swooped, bat-like and there came a hideous scream. It was not I whom he sought. A wretched slave, out of curiosity, or perhaps bribed by others, had contrived to stay behind his fellows when they swarmed out for their short hours of sleep. Hanging by one hand, he was creeping up the metal sides of a great container, so that he might gaze in.

I saw Elvideus assume his human form. From his eyes darted a sombre ray which seemed to transfix the unhappy wretch, so that he stood hypnotized, whilst his master approached him, took him by the hand and led him once again to the container, saying gently – 'Your curiosity shall be rewarded – LOOK IN.'

Trembling and moaning, the slave once more laid his hand upon the dreaded and sinister vessel. I saw the magician touch a small knob upon its side, and at once, with a fierce hiss, lightning shot from the shafts projecting from its upper edge.

And the slave? He was *not*! Only a blackened, shrivelled mass still clinging horribly to the enchanted metal, showed where flesh and blood had been.

Appalled, I gazed upon the magician, standing there triumphant. His aura was a reddish black, luminous with evil power. But his eyes were a brilliant blue, keen, piercing and cold. Lust for power, frigidly callous, shone in that intelligent face.

I saw him raise his hands, summoning a strange god. *'Fohat! Fohat!' he cried. 'To thee, I give my homage. Grant me strength! Teach me to split the vibrating particles of matter so that I and I alone may be the master of the world and the planets!'

As he ceased to intone this sinister evocation, there came a tremendous peal as of thunder, and a vast zig-zag spear of lightning. The pit reverberated, and the magician outlined in the unholy flame, bowed his head in worship.

He touched another knob, and the great monster began to whir and hum, vibrating and swaying with some awesome, leashed-in force whose terror and power impacted on me – yes, even on my etheric body, which quivered and shrank.

Awe was upon me, for the harnessed force must be more than earthly! Was this man or god?

I gathered up my spiritual resources, as this hellish breath blew upon them. I was in mortal danger – not material, for he had not noticed my presence (or – had he? For he was very subtle!) but the fearful inner danger of spiritual wreck.

Calling urgently upon the Unknown Master, I withdrew, blending and blurring away as I had been taught to do, outwards and upwards into the pure air of dawn.

There, in a little leafy copse, I prayed, and slowly and carefully re-entered my body and awoke.

---

* Name given by ancients to electric light.

125

I found you very agitated, for something of the grim terror of that pit had reached you.

You cried, 'We must now find Noasa! I heard today from a wandering goatherd, strange rumours of him, that he has received a warning of disaster and plans to build a place of safety. As your messages came, my whole being bade me give you this counsel!'

And so, we prepared for our long journey over the plains and forest and up the great mountain to the north of Atlantis – the only one not of volcanic origin.

For Elvideus had dug his pit on the very doorstep of one of the greatest of the seemingly extinct volcanoes which rose from the Atlantean plain.

We set off without many attendants, only two body slaves and a runner, on the long trek across the smiling land of Atlantis, over the plain and up the lower slopes of the Adaan Mountains.

Having climbed 2,000 feet, we came upon a long and narrow wooded plateau, behind which rose the main range. There, so we were told, the great seer Noasa was engaged in some form of meditation, and, so it was rumoured, in some strange form of building.

It seemed we were expected, for we were at once led into the presence of the Seer. Once more those piercing eyes sought into our inner selves, through the veils of Personality to the Ego within.

'It is well,' said he. 'Here you must stay; do not seek to return for the hour of doom is very near. Come with me and see my work.'

He led us along a path to a meadow and there we beheld a huge erection which vastly puzzled us. For few in our Atlantis had seen a great ship. Small boats and barges we had for our rather shallow smooth flowing rivers, and there were vague legends of great floating houses, yet few would have recognized, in this strange building with its flat surface, tapering to so narrow an edge that its bulk had to be supported by scaffolding, a ship in course of construction.

When the prophet making a sign in the air cried: 'Here the few shall take refuge from the flood of destruction,' we understood nothing of his meaning. But we did understand that we were invited to stay and become his disciples, and so we became members of the encampment and entered into its daily routine of meditation and hard labour, all with a sense of urgency of racing against time, so acute that the Seer himself would frequently mingle amongst us using the axe or hone at our side.

Little by little the erection grew. Upon the flat surface rose tiers of galleries and finally upon the whole was placed a roof, like a box.

In all there was a company of about forty, men and women, working at this strange task, of whom ten were underlings from the slave class, but each in his minor way, clairvoyant.

Sometimes when there was heavy lifting to do, some huge tree to transport upwards, the Seer would come, and gathering all these humble workers, would make a sign, whereupon all would stand with shut eyes and emptied faces, whilst he, with intense concentration, would gaze steadily upon the log, holding out his two hands with fingers out-pointing, one hand behind the other from the forehead outwards. Slowly the inert mass would quiver and rise suspended in mid air. A body of helpers would swiftly mount the scaffolding, lasso the log with ropes and haul it into position.

Day in, day out, we laboured and ever the sense of impending need grew. At first there were times within the day when the Seer would call us apart and instruct us in the wisdom, but with the passing of the days, he could not tear himself away from the ship and finally took his hut and slept near by.

At last, after she was given the final coat of resinous oil there she lay, a huge ship, looking fantastically strange, perched there high on the slopes of a mountain.

One day a party arrived to parley with the Seer. Elvideus, whose power enabled him to see clairvoyantly the 'temple' being built by his rival, but who could not divine its purpose, for, to the being blinded by illusion, the future presents itself in the light of his phantasy, would not tolerate the suspicion that another prophet might be stealing a march on him. By now he had come out into the open as a would-be ruler of the world. By a ruthless act of magic he had slain the High Priest at the altar, and taken his place. All trembled before him.

The Seer addressed the visitors, his tall figure, outlined in the red of a stormy sunset, seeming to expand to twice its height and his glowing eyes emitting a steady beam of power.

'Flee, flee! The hour is at hand! Heed my words before the pit of fire, the deluge of hail engulfs you and yours. No act of man can avert this, for the forces of evil are uppermost. Earth rejects them and the waters must cleanse!'

So great was the power of his spirit that terror seized them and they fled. Later, I heard by occult means, that all but three had heeded the warning and had set off across the mountains, and after frightful hardships had come to resting place in what is now Iceland.

There came a dawn when the Seer aroused us with urgent words.

'Gather together such trifles as you need on a long journey and bind them firmly upon your backs, and come to the clearing behind the ship.'

This done with haste, for there was that in his manner which filled us with a sense of impending doom, he adjured us to pray, uttering the Sacred Word – the clarion call to the spheres.

'Today,' he cried, 'Elvideus, spawn of evil, has determined to test the ultimate result of his researches in the pit. This is the moment against whose dire outcome I have been striving this many months!'

And so, chanting evocations, and weaving in solemn rhythm upon the grass the mystic figures which repel evil, we waited for we knew not what.

Even Nature seemed subdued: no bird sang, the sun was veiled in black thunder clouds, the gracious land of Atlantis seemed to mourn its doom.

From this mountain plateau where the great ship lay, there was a clear, uninterrupted view over the green plains, with the river and its tributaries like leaden threads winding across them, and losing itself in the far distance in a mass of wild, almost virgin forest, and with the two volcanic peaks, quiescent and harmless, flanking the outermost boundaries of the capital, whose gleaming white houses we could faintly distinguish. On its southern boundary lay the dark blur which was the great wood within which was hidden Elvideus' pit.

'At the sign of my hand,' warned the Seer, 'fall down upon the ground, burying your faces in the earth!'

Intent and taut we waited. I prayed and you, pale of face, sat with shut eyes, seeming entranced.

Presently you began to murmur, 'I have projected myself to the city: they seem to be preparing for a great ceremony. Elvideus in all his robes, is standing at the gate of his pit and all the people are on their knees before him. I see a sort of lever by his side. I can't get it clearly – it seems to be attaching to some thread leading down...down – oh ye gods, I glimpsed your monster mystery! It hums and vibrates. There is a red-black aura of evil everywhere: the atmosphere is frightful!'

You emerged, you seemed faint and choking, but I laid my hands on yours and you revived.

Suddenly the voice of the Seer rang out: 'Be ready – it comes!'

Even with his last word, a blinding light of terrific force and velocity seemed to rise from the far-off city and envelop us, with a sensation as if we had been struck a sharp blow. We fell upon the ground as a great column of inky smoke rose high, high, almost beyond vision. As we fell flat, the earth rocked and seemed to sway with the force of an impact which we could sense even on our distant mountain.

There was a minute of silence, dead, sinister. I opened my eyes. You were sitting up, with an almost insane smile upon your lips. You stared into the distance and muttered!

The black cloud poured outwards and lowered upon us. In the strange stillness as if all sound had been destroyed, there came a deep groan from one of the younger men. He swayed upon his knees, livid of face.

The Seer stretched forth his hand and touched the sufferer saying, 'No real harm here. We are too far away. Wait and be ready. Look upon what was Atlantis!'

And now, into that stillness, empty, as if all motion, all sound, had been sucked away by the flame of searing light, there came a rending and a roaring, a cracking and a shivering. The earth was splitting into a dozen fissures. It sank, it heaved, as if struck by a giant axe.

'The volcano! See, the volcano!' you gasped.

Out from its silent crater poured a belching column of smoke, followed by flame, and down its slopes gushed red-hot lava, shining out in the surrounding black smoke like a red cloth on a black table. The rending and the quivering of the plain went on, and a spate of huge rocks flew out of the mountain's bowels, battering down upon what had been a stately city.

We had flung ourselves upon the ground which even so far away, heaved and shook, but not dangerously. As the first impact of the rending terror decreased, it steadied and we were able to stand upright, but our trembling was such that our knees were like jelly beneath us.

'Into the ship!' thundered the Seer, and we turned, groping our way in the drifts of darkness which blew hither and thither like mist on a mountain top, and swarmed on to the lower deck of the new ship.

And now came the rain – yet rain is no word for the bucketing deluge of sheeted water which flung itself upon us from the sky, as we crawled into shelter.

The terrified animals, long ago safely attached in their stables, squealed and whinnied and the air around seemed filled with the shrieking of many demons. In the midst of this concatenation of noise, could be heard one steady high-pitched whining roar whose origin we could not guess.

'It is the water elementals!' cried the Seer. 'They cleanse and purify, washing away the pus of evil. Praise them and bless!'

Deep was our darkness and isolated terror, but the voice of the Seer rose like the peal of an organ, exhorting and praying.

For twenty-four hours, each hour a lifetime of horror and amazement, the deluge lasted. Then, relieved, we saw the overhanging blanket of mist begin to lift and the torrent of rain to slacken so that we could view, if but indistinctly, the distant plain.

Over the city, a pall, funeral pall in very truth, of mist, still hung. The fertile plain was now split in twain by a tremendous gaping fissure extending as far as eye could see through the distant forest belt.

The volcano had calmed a little, but a steady stream of smoke and lava oozed from the crater, with an occasional spurt of roaring explosion.

The waters of time are like a smooth-flowing river, viewed as I do, in a vast retrospect, but here and there a giant bubble rises seething to the surface, bursts and is gone. Such, it seems, was Atlantis! Trembling, we gazed at what had been our home, and some of us cried out that we must go down and seek news of our families and our properties.

But the Seer admonished us, 'Enough of such folly: the end is yet to come! Be prepared!!'

Scarcely had he finished, when into the midst of the wild, terrifying sounds which still smote our ears, there came another, at first distant, ever approaching, with somewhat of immense menace in its soft roar. It seemed like the rushing of an ocean, and at first we could not think whence it came. A gale was rising, so abnormally strong and swift that we were hard put to it to stand upon the decks.

Suddenly with a cry of awed amazement, the Seer's youngest nephew, a warrior already developing much occult power, called out, 'The tide! the tide! See it, over the forest!'

We looked and saw what surely no man has seen before or since. A vast wall of water was rolling along the deep fissure which cleft Atlantis in twain. It approached till the fissure was a raging torrent rushing higher and nearer to the surface of the plain.

Dumb with horrid fear, we watched the first exploring wave break over the surface of the land around, followed by another and another, gentle at first like the playful pat of a tiger. Soon, the whole mass of water was over and spreading across the land.

'Be ready!' once more called the Seer.

Aghast, we saw in the half light, as the choking fog cleared away before the driving wind, the grey-black seething wall of water spilling over the fissure, creeping out, out over the ruined pastures ever deeper, ever swifter, engulfing trees and rocks and homesteads, sweeping away cattle, sheep, horses, chattering monkeys, seeping slowly nearer the distant city, rising, rising –

Again the incredible, bucketing deluge began and with it, the

131

crashing rumble of thunder, with the murky darkness lit up by jagged arrows of lightning which seemed, in some strange willed way, to streak across the sky and focus on that spot where had lain the pit, whence it had been invoked.

The tempo quickened. With hideous menace, the waters, now a vast bubbling waste, engulfed our mountain's lower slopes. Of the volcanoes, only the high peaks remained, with craters still ejecting red-hot lava which plunged into the waters with a sizzling roar, sending out clouds of boiling steam.

Again the Seer cried, 'Be ready: stand to the oars!'

The long strong oars were laid in the rowlocks, and the strongest of our young men leapt into place and leaned over, waiting.

The waters rose: now only the crowns of our pine spinney were visible: now the first creeping arms slapped round our keel.

Slowly, slowly, they crept up our ship's flanks, and then, with one strong pushing of our oars, we took off. We were afloat on that seething ocean which had swallowed all the world we knew!

Night blended with the brooding dark of that day as we rowed slowly, amidst huge waves, which, unfilled by the abnormal winds now abating, caught our ship.

The Seer, withdrawn into some inner world, stood unmoving, like a carven figure head, holding the helm, yet never moving it, for by some magic, our vessel kept an undeviating course towards we knew not what.

The wind died down, the clouds drifted away and a shaft of silver light danced upon the water, as the moon at its full peered over the horizon, charging the waters with liquid magic. Star after star added their pin points of light and a great peace flowed down upon the waste of waters which was all that was left of Atlantis. Now and then a corpse floated past, staring-eyed and green in the unearthly light. Luminous shapes, the newly dead, flowed by, seeking their own. Some lit upon the ship and rested in our midst.

One by one, the weary band lay down to sleep, leaving only the oarsmen drowsily plying their oars.

Slumber was upon the ship, but the Seer kept watch all night.

Once, opening my eyes at dawn, I saw that his cheeks were wet with tears.

In the morning we awoke and opened our eyes upon a sullen grey desert of water, and this we woke to for over forty days. To us, unused to the ocean, for such it was – the new Atlantic Ocean – the ordeal was severe. But we had learnt to carry peace within ourselves and this serenity made a triple armour.

At last, one morning, watching the Seer as he stood at the helm, I saw a circling speck above his head which hovered and alighted. It was a bird – a huge sea bird, which snatched a fish from the deck and soared away with eerie shrieks. Another came and still another: they followed the ship, screaming over our top deck, shy, yet bold in hunger.

'This,' cried the Seer, 'means land – watch for a sign!'

There was about us a thick white mist which cut off all view, till one morning, it broke suddenly, and there loomed upon us a giant rock, stark and precipitous. No way of landing there – yet it was the good earth! Gazing to the right across the ocean we saw far off, separated from the rock by an expanse of water, a coast-line, with surfy shore fringing a range of golden-brown mountains.

'Through this channel,' said the Seer, 'whose guard and bastion this rock shall ever be, must we sail into the mid-Earth sea. Our way lies before us and soon we shall find land.'

Some would have murmured. Weary to the marrow of water, they wished to make directly for the coast opposite the rock, but even as the Seer spoke, there came another mighty tidal wave which seized our ship irresistibly and bore it, bobbing and bowing, yet always afloat, on its swirling breast.

So high was this wave that it well-nigh submerged even the immense rock, which we soon left far behind, as we floated on between two faintly distinguishable lines of coast.

Came a morning, at long last, when the speed of the giant tidal wave slackened, the land drew nearer, and just as gently as we had set out, one powerful wave deposited us high and dry upon a stretch of rocky earth at the base of a precipitous rocky peak.

In the morning, to our immense surprise, we found that we

had come to land as we had departed; high on the slopes of a mountain. Its flanks, from which the waves had now receded, stretched far below us, with a narrow strip of surf-beaten coast between us and the now brilliantly sun-lit blue water. The drenched and sodden earth steamed in the almost tropical heat, and strange shaped trees which we were later to know as palms, shaking themselves like a wet dog, swayed and sighed in the still powerful wind.

'Here,' cried the Seer, 'we shall rest, but not remain. Step upon land – the flood is ended!'

Blessing with uplifted hand the ship whose strong body had brought us out of destruction into safety, he led the way.

We were indeed in a strange and fantastic plight, perched like birds three thousand feet up the side of a mountain. Our ship, beached upon an alp similar to its place of departure, looked naked and forlorn, bereft of the element on which it rode so gracefully. Already as the wind increased, it was tilting and keeling over.

We got rapidly to work, bringing out stores and tents, freeing the wearied animals and driving them down the rough slopes of the mountain to the coastal plain below, where we rigged up a rough encampment and refreshed ourselves with wild fruits, dates, nuts, wild corn and sassafras.

Here for three days we rested. Afterwards, as it was not the hottest part of the year, we trekked steadily to the east along the shores of this sea which was bluer than the deep borders of our High Priest's robe.

On the fifty-second day of our trek, after an ordered twenty-four-hours fast, on a clear, starlit night, with the moon at the full, the Seer called us to an assembly on a rock-strewn beach. It was a ceremonial invocation.

Holding fingertips, we weaved, within the borders of a star-shaped figure demarcated by triple lines beyond which was sprinkled salt, an intricate pattern of swaying rhythm, chanting the Sacred Word very deep within so that it filled our bodies like the humming of a bee caught in a churn, the high rocks around resounded with the organ notes of the spheres, and the very sky vibrated to the potent inner sound.

Suddenly, the Seer stopped dead, and lifting his hand, pointed towards you and me.

'Andama and Persamen!' he cried. 'Disciples and friends, for you now comes the parting: your destiny leads you further – for you, is more adventure. Yonder is my resting-place, a land of mystery fed by a sacred river which waters the desert. But you must once more set sail, and seek a distant shore, and there after long wandering, you will find your own. It is farewell! Round yonder creek, there is a boat – it is for you!'

With solemn ceremonies of farewell, commending us to universal harmony and peace, he led us by the hand like children to a hidden creek beyond a jutting wall of rock, and there lay a small but sturdy sailing-boat. How she came there, we could not guess!

Loading within it our few private possessions and a good store of food, and followed only by the faithful three who had come from our home in Atlantis, we set sail, leaving behind for ever those loved companions of the flood.

Yet to those who are upon the Path, no human tie must bind: all must be detachable, for the short span of incarnation is less than a speck of dust in the desert of time. And the Seer we could visit in sleep: this much he promised. We should never be bereft of his guiding wisdom.

And so we sailed together over the deep blue mid-earth sea, and of our adventures in the long voyage, of the ships we saw and their strange mariners, there is no space to tell, and indeed, the records are not clear, for this part of our life was not important, in Eternity.

Yes – in these records imprinted on the thought-woof of our Ego, certain patches stand out vividly, clear-cut 'purple patches', where far-reaching events were being lived through, but between whiles come long tracks of grey or dimly patterned web, hard to disentangle. The lives of many people, I find, hold little but this grey weft, but yours and mine are a series of lurid, outstanding patterns of adventure, from the earliest I can glimpse.

Sailing in our little boat on this smooth and smiling sea, borne on a gentle breeze, we drifted through many days, till at last, when our food was gone, we came upon a creek, in a lonely sandy shore, and there we stepped upon the land knowing that our sea voyage was over and that never again should we set sail upon the ocean, or even see it.

Therefore we solemnly bade farewell to the silken waters we had come to love, and ever since, in all our incarnations, you and I have loved the sea.

And so we were at last ashore, for ever. The country was wild: in the distance, beyond the flat and evil-smelling sandy shore, we saw, for the first time, those mighty mountains ice-peaked in gleaming sunshine which are now known as the Suleimans, with beyond them the Hindu Kush. Thither we knew it was our fate to wander. Setting up our little tent of skins, we lay that night upon the shores of Asia, which was to be our home for several lives upon Earth.

There, above the little sandy creek, we came upon a spring of pure sweet water and from it led a narrow beaten track steeply mounting from the shore.

Destiny had indeed led her children, for in the morning as we gratefully drank the sweet water and ate the last of our store of food, there appeared over the brow of the sloping track, two riders, soberly clad, with turbans and flowing robes, who sat upon beasts more strange than we could have imagined in a dream. These creatures, camels as you call them, were to become very familiar in the days to come, but never much beloved!

Behind the two riders we saw litters borne by slaves, on which lay veiled women and a train of loaded pack-mules.

When we arose, they stood amazed, and the tallest, an elderly man, approached us.

Suddenly, he fell upon his knees and pointing to the sacred ring of the amulet that you wore, he cried, 'Who be ye that wear the great seal of wisdom? We are your servants! We go to trade silks for gold in Ind. You are welcome to all we have.'

So we travelled with the caravan, passing through much strange country as the great peaks drew nearer and the path wilder. After long and toilsome climbing, we entered a stern and terrible pass between grey-brown boulder-strewn precipices; the only way, our host said, through country infested with fierce and greedy tribesmen into the land of Ind.

Finally we emerged upon a plain where we came upon a city with domed palaces and flat-roofed houses. The people were dark-skinned and slender with gentle lustrous eyes, but there was much dirt and disease, it seemed to us, used to advanced Atlantis, where the laws of nature were understood and obeyed.

The merchant led us to a palace whose very doors were studded with gold and jewels, and guarded by keen-eyed fierce spearsmen. There, in an inner room, we were led to the presence of a prince before whose sandalled feet our friend and his servants fell, kissing the ground.

This was not our way; we stood erect. At once wrath distorted the faces of the prince's attendants, who made to attack us. By the force of our thought we held them transfixed, swords in air. They gaped amazed, whilst the prince, who was young and wise of face, arose and moved towards us, took our hands and, bidding all others depart, led us to his throne so that he might hear our story.

It was the beginning of a long and fruitful friendship.

We were accepted as magicians from afar, under the prince's protection. For ten years we worked mightily in the founding of a school of the wisdom, where those who were fitted might share our knowledge. Hundreds came and profited exceedingly, for it was the nature of this race to sense the unseen. They had already some glimmerings of the Way, but the giant idols they worshipped gave forth little of the truth of the Spirit. Yet as always when light shines in dark places, crawling maggots were revealed.

These idols had their priests who brooded over their fall from dignity, yet were powerless to avenge themselves whilst this prince held the reins.

But there came a day, ten years after our arrival, when he took a fever, and our inner knowledge told us his days were numbered.

The priests came and challenged us to save him by our arts. This we strove to do and would have succeeded had not one of these jealous and ruthless prelates placed poison in his cup, helped by a treacherous woman slave against whom we had warned him in vain.

When he lay dead, the priests accused us of fraud and we

knew our work in this place was ended. By our power, we fled by night and together retraced the journey through the pass.

After long wanderings, the record shows that we died together (not unhappily, for unearthly visions illuminated our end), lost in the deserts of Araby.

FURTHER READING

Introduction
Sheldrake, Rupert, *A New Science of Life* (J.P.Tarcher, 1981)
Weber, Renée, *Dialogues With Scientists and Sages* (Routledge & Kegan Paul, 1986)

Chapter 1, Part 1
Gleick, James, *Chaos* (Sphere Books, 1988)
Hall, Nina, ed., *The New Scientist Guide to Chaos* (Penguin Books, 1991)
Stewart, Ian, *Does God Play Dice?* (Blackwell, 1990)

Chapter 1, Part 2
Buckminster Fuller, R., *Critical Path* (Hutchinson, 1983)
Capra, Fritjof, *The Tao of Physics* (Flamingo, 1990)
Kauffman, Stuart A., *The Origins of Order: Self-organization and Selection in Evolution* (OUP, 1993)

Chapter 2
Bennett, John G., *Gurdjieff – Making a New World* (Turnstone Books, 1976)
Joseph, G.G., *The Crest of the Peacock, Non-European Roots of Mathematics* (Penguin Books, 1992)
Walker, Kenneth, *A Study of Gurdjieff's Teachings* (Jonathon Cape, 1957)
Wells, David G., *The Penguin Dictionary of Curious and Interesting Numbers*, (Penguin Books, 1987)

Chapter 3
Alexandersson, Olaf, *Living Water* (Gateway Books, 1990)
Ash, David A. (see page 97), *The Vortex* (Available in pre-publication form, price £15, from the author at 4, Western House, Station Road, Totnes, Devon)
Bird, Christopher, *Divining* (M. & J. Raven, 1990)

Fountain International, magazines and booklets available from PO Box 52, Torquay TQ2 8PE

Iyengar, B.K.S., *Light on Yoga* (George Allen & Unwin, 1965)

Underwood, Guy, *The Pattern of the Past* (Museum, 1969 – Abacus 1972, Sphere Books)

Chapter 4

Gilbert, Alice, *Philip in the Spheres* (The Aquarian Press, 1952)

Lovelock, J.E., *Gaia* (Oxford, 1979, reprinted 1991)

Chapter 5

Davies, Paul and Gribbin, John, *The Matter Myth* (Viking, 1991, The Penguin Group)

Fauvel, John and Flood, Raymond, eds, *Let Newton Be* (OUP, 1988)

Penrose, Roger, *The Emperor's New Mind* (Vintage, 1990)

Wade, David, *Crystal & Dragon – The Cosmic Two-step* (Green Books, 1991)

Westfall, Richard S., *Never at Rest* (CUP)

The Society of Metaphysicians Ltd (see page 111), Archers Court, Stonestile Lane, The Ridge, Hastings TN35 4PG.
Tel: 01424 751577.

The President, Dr J.J. Williamson, welcomes enquiries regarding membership and research activities. A large selection of relevant books is available.